SPECIAL NEEDS in the early years

Learning difficulties

IDENTIFYING AND SUPPORTING NEEDS • ACTIVITIES COVERING EARLY LEARNING GOALS • WORKING WITH PARENTS

DR HANNAH MORTIMER

Author
Dr Hannah Mortimer

Editor
Clare Miller

Assistant Editor
Saveria Mezzana

Series Designers
Sarah Rock/Anna Oliwa

Designer
Paul Cheshire

Illustrations
Cathy Hughes

Cover artwork
Claire Henley

Acknowledgements
The publishers gratefully acknowledge permission to reproduce the following
copyright material:

Brenda Williams for the use of 'Out of my window' by Brenda Williams © 2002, Brenda
Williams, previously unpublished.
Qualifications and Curriculum Authority for the use of extracts from the
QCA/DfEE document *Curriculum Guidance for the Foundation Stage*
© 2000, Qualifications and Curriculum Authority.

The publishers wish to thank Makaton Vocabulary Development Project for their help in
reproducing the Makaton illustrations in this book.
Every effort has been made to trace copyright holders and the publishers apologize for any
inadvertent omissions.

Text © 2002, Hannah Mortimer
© 2002, Scholastic Ltd

Designed using Adobe Pagemaker

Published by Scholastic Ltd, Villiers House,
Clarendon Avenue, Leamington Spa, Warwickshire CV32 5PR
Visit our website at www.scholastic.co.uk

Printed by Alden Group Ltd, Oxford

2 3 4 5 6 7 8 9 0   2 3 4 5 6 7 8 9 0 1

British Library Cataloguing-in-Publication Data A catalogue record for this book is
available from the British Library.

ISBN 0 439 01973 7

Learning difficulties

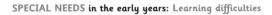

INTRODUCTION

In every early years group there are children learning and developing at many different stages. This book provides you with practical ideas for including children with learning difficulties in the activities at your setting.

The aims of the series

There is now a new, revised *Code of Practice* for the identification and assessment of special educational needs. This series aims to provide guidance to early years practitioners on how to meet and monitor special educational needs (SEN) under the new Code. In addition, the QCA document *Curriculum Guidance for the Foundation Stage* emphasizes the key role that early years practitioners play in identifying needs and responding to them quickly. While it is generally accepted that an inclusive approach is the best one for all the children concerned, it is still useful to have guidance on what an inclusive early years curriculum might actually 'look like' in practice.

The *Special Needs in the Early Years* series includes books on helping children with most kinds of special needs:

- behavioural and emotional difficulties
- speech and language difficulties
- learning difficulties
- physical and co-ordination difficulties
- autistic spectrum difficulties
- medical difficulties
- sensory difficulties.

An additional handbook for the whole series, *Special Needs Handbook*, provides general guidance and more detail on how to assess, plan for, teach and monitor children with SEN in early years settings.

Most groups will at some point include children who have learning difficulties or general developmental delay. This book will help all early years professionals to recognize and understand such difficulties and to provide inclusive activities for the children involved. Market research has shown that early years practitioners would welcome practical advice and guidelines for children with learning difficulties.

Background information

Chapter 1 provides an introduction to requirements under the revised *Code of Practice* for SEN as it relates to children who have learning difficulties. This is a brief guide only, with reference made to the series handbook for more information. There is also a reminder of the requirements of the QCA Early Learning Goals and Curriculum Guidelines across each Area of Learning. The need for individual education plans for those children who have SEN will be introduced with information on what it means to meet SEN in an inclusive way. There are also pointers for developing positive partnerships and relationships with carers and

families and an introduction to some of the outside agencies which you may be required to liaise with.

Chapter 2 looks more closely at the needs of children who have general learning difficulties. It answers questions such as: What kinds of conditions and needs are covered in the book? How do learning difficulties arise and how might they be identified? What do these difficulties mean for the child and what are the educational implications? Advice is also provided on looking for special opportunities for promoting development, linked to the early years curriculum. There are ideas for trying a range of approaches and making use of the full range of resources and activities available in your setting.

Areas of Learning

Chapters 3 to 8 are six activity chapters, each related to one of the QCA Areas of Learning: Personal, social and emotional development; Communication, language and literacy; Mathematical development; Knowledge and understanding of the world; Physical development and Creative development. Each chapter contains ten activities, each having a learning objective for all the children (with or without SEN) and an individual learning target for any child who might have any one of a range of learning difficulties. The activities will target different kinds of difficulties in the hope that early years workers will become able to develop a flexible approach to planning inclusive activities, dipping into the ideas which pepper these chapters. It is suggested that you read through them all for their general ideas, and then select activities as and when you need them as part of your general curriculum planning.

Each activity also provides information on appropriate group size, a list of what is needed, a description of what to do, any special support which might be necessary for the child with SEN, ideas for extending the activity for more able children and suggestions for links with home. These guidelines can be used flexibly, in a manner that is relevant to the particular needs of the children in your setting.

Though this book relates to the early years and SEN procedures followed in England, the general guidance on individual planning, positive behaviour management and activities can be applied equally well to early years settings in Scotland, Wales and Northern Ireland.

Normal learning development

Though each child is a unique and special individual, children's development appears to follow a very similar pathway. There are certain recognizable steps in a child's development that are referred to as their 'developmental milestones'. It is helpful to spend some time looking at how developmental milestones typically progress in each of the six Areas of Learning.

Children described as experiencing 'learning difficulties' are likely to be reaching developmental milestones later than most of their peers. In particular, their cognitive (or thinking) skills might be delayed. This is likely to affect their language, numerical skills and acquisition of knowledge. Quite often, personal and social skills might also be immature. Creative ability and physical skills may or may not be delayed as well.

SPECIAL NEEDS in the early years: Learning difficulties

Personal, social and emotional development

Most one-year-olds are still very dependent on a caring adult for their confidence and are likely to find separation difficult unless they have become attached to their alternative carer. The two-year-old is ready to explore and play, so long as an interested adult is close by, though most of the play is in parallel to other children. The three-year-old is beginning to play co-operatively with another child for a short time and this is developed when the child is four. Four-year-olds are likely to talk of their 'friends' and these are usually the children with whom they have played most that session rather than any long-standing relationship. Confidence begins to emerge as the child meets new situations, experiments, experiences success and therefore tries again next time.

Communication, language and literacy

Most children are speaking in a few single words by the time they reach their first birthday. Over their second year, they quickly acquire more words and begin to build these into short phrases. The two-year-old can follow very simple instructions with one or two pieces of information such as 'show me your *nose*' or 'go upstairs for your *shoes*'. Questions begin to be asked, and these increase greatly when the child is three. Children begin to be able to speak in plurals and in negatives and to use describing words. First attempts at mark-making come when the child is one, moving on to letter-like shapes by the time the child is two to three. The three-year-old loves to chatter and the four-year-old is developing all the skills necessary for maintaining a conversation with a friend. The four-year-old is also beginning to use language to imagine and to think.

Mathematical development

Three-year-olds are usually able to tell you which of two objects is 'bigger' or 'smaller'. Later, the concepts long and short, and high and low also emerge. Colour-naming typically develops over the third to fourth year and counting by rote comes at about the same time, with one-to-one correspondence developing at four to five years of age. Children can usually copy and name very simple shapes at between three and four years of age. They begin to recognize the numerals associated to their age first, and learn to count best when moving to the count (such as counting up steps).

Knowledge and understanding of the world

This area of learning blossoms in the three-year-old, expressed and developed through active questioning. Quite often, the same questions will be asked over and over, almost as if to check out that today's answer is indeed the same as yesterday. 'What' questions are asked first, then the important 'Why' questions, followed by 'When' and 'How'. The child's knowledge and understanding will be linked to the amount of time and experience given by interested adults, and to the child's capacity to assimilate, or build in, the new information with their own

experiences. Concepts are learned by making links between words and actions or experiences.

Physical development

This area of learning improves with practice and confidence. The two-year-old still runs with a fairly wide gait and has a poor spatial and physical awareness, frequently stumbling if they have not looked where they are going. In time, running becomes more fluent, and balancing is achieved while moving. The three-year-old is beginning to be able to balance on one leg for a short time, and is climbing and jumping with growing confidence. Most four-year-olds learn to pedal a wheeled toy and can change direction as they run.

Creative development

Creative expression can be enjoyed at any age. Even the youngest child, or a child with severe learning difficulties, can enjoy touch, feel, colour, music and movement. In this area of learning, activities should be inclusive to all and should aim to encourage the children's natural expression.

Using resources in the nursery

The activities described in this book suggest ways to make use of a wide range of resources and materials available to most early years settings. There are ideas for art and craft, story time, physical play and for exploring and finding out. There is a focus on the value of circle-time activities with young children, since these have been shown to be very effective in building children's self-esteem and confidence and in teaching them how to demonstrate new skills within a group. A regular music circle time, for example, can enhance looking, listening and confidence both within the circle time and beyond. Many of the activities found in this book involve a musical approach.

Links with home

All the activities suggest ways of keeping closely in touch with home. By sharing activities with parents and carers, practitioners can also play a role in helping the parents or carers of a child who has learning difficulties to follow approaches at home which will offer continued encouragement to the child.

Providing special support

You need to make sure that the child with SEN is accessing the full range of your early years provision. Clearly this cannot happen if the child is isolated in any way or withdrawn from the group regularly, and this is another reason for collecting ideas for inclusive group activities. 'Support' does not mean individual one-to-one attention. Instead, it can mean playing alongside a child and teaching them in small groups, or simply watching on so as to encourage new learning and stay 'one step ahead' of any problem areas. You will find suggestions for doing this in Chapter 2.

LEGAL REQUIREMENTS

This chapter explains your legal requirements towards children with learning difficulties. You will find ideas for planning and monitoring their progress and for working with parents and carers and with other professionals.

The *Code of Practice* for SEN

The SEN *Code of Practice* is a guide for school governors, registered early years providers and Local Education Authorities about the practical help they can give to children with special educational needs. It recommends that schools and early years providers should identify children's needs and take action, working with parents and carers, to meet those needs as early as possible. The aim is to enable all pupils with SEN to reach their full potential, to be included fully in their school communities and to make a successful transition to adulthood. The Code gives guidance to schools and early years providers, but it does not tell them what they must do in every case.

In 1996, the DfEE stated that all pre-school providers in the voluntary and non-maintained sectors who registered to redeem vouchers should also have regard to the *Code of Practice*. This continues to be the case for groups registering with the Local Education Authority (LEA) under the Early Years and Childcare Development Plan. There is now a new, revised SEN *Code of Practice* and this is described more fully in the handbook accompanying this series, *Special Needs Handbook*.

The *Code of Practice* principles

What are the underlying principles for early years settings? All children have a right to a broad and balanced curriculum which enables them to make maximum progress towards the Early Learning Goals. Each early years practitioner must recognize, identify and meet SEN within their setting. There will be a range of need and a range of provision to meet that need. Most children with SEN will be in a local mainstream early years group or class, even those who have 'statements of SEN'. Carers, children, early years settings, and support services should work as partners in planning for and meeting SEN. The *Code of Practice* is designed to enable special educational needs to be identified early and to be addressed. These SEN will normally be met in the local mainstream setting, though some children may need extra consideration or help to be able to access the early years curriculum fully in the setting. There is more detailed information about requirements under the SEN *Code of Practice* in the series handbook.

Early Years Action Plus

It is recognized that good practice can take many forms and early years providers are encouraged to adopt a flexible and a graduated response to the SEN of individual children. Such an approach recognizes that there is a continuum of SEN and, where necessary, brings increasing specialist expertise on board if the child is experiencing ongoing difficulties.

Once a child's SEN have been identified, the providers should intervene through 'Early Years Action'. When reviewing the child's progress and the help they are receiving, the provider might decide to seek alternative approaches to learning through the outside support services. These interventions are known as 'Early Years Action Plus'. This is characterized by the involvement of specialists from outside the setting.

The Special Educational Needs Co-ordinator (SENCO) continues to take a leading role, working closely with the member of staff responsible for the child, and:

● draws on advice from outside specialists, for example Early Years Support Teachers or Educational Psychologists;

● ensures that the child and his or her carers are consulted and kept informed;

● ensures that an individual education plan (IEP) is drawn up, incorporating the specialist advice, and that this is included in the curriculum planning for the whole setting;

● with outside specialists, monitors and reviews the child's progress;

● keeps the Head of the setting informed.

SEN statements

For a very few children, the help provided by Early Years Action Plus will still not be sufficient to ensure satisfactory progress, even when it has run over several review periods. The provider, the external professional and the parents or carers may then decide to ask the LEA to consider carrying out a statutory assessment of the child's SEN.

The LEA must decide quickly whether or not it has the 'evidence' to indicate that a statutory assessment is necessary for a child. It is then responsible for co-ordinating a statutory assessment and will call for the various reports that it requires. These will be from: the early years teacher (usually a support teacher, early years practitioner or LEA nursery teacher); an educational psychologist; a doctor (who will also gather 'evidence' from any speech and language therapist involved) and the Social Services department (if involved). Parents and carers will also be asked to submit their own views and evidence.

Once the LEA has collected the evidence, it might decide to issue a 'statement of SEN' for the child. Only children with severe and long-standing SEN go on to receive a statement – about two per cent of children. There are various rights of appeal in the cases of disagreement, and the LEA can provide information about these.

Requirements of the Early Learning Goals

Registered early years providers are also expected to deliver this broad and balanced curriculum across the six Areas of Learning as defined in the *Curriculum Guidance for the Foundation stage* (QCA). This paves the way for children's early learning to be followed through into Baseline Assessment measures on entry to school and into National Curriculum assessment for school-age children. It is intended that the integration of these three areas will contribute to the earlier identification of children who are experiencing difficulties in making progress in their learning.

Trouble has been taken to set the Early Learning Goals in context so that they are considered as an aid to planning ahead rather than as an early years curriculum to replace 'learning through play'. Effective early years education requires both a relevant curriculum and practitioners who understand it and are able to implement it. To this end, practical examples of Stepping Stones towards the Early Learning Goals are provided in the detailed *Curriculum Guidance for the Foundation Stage* document. In this book, you will find that each activity is linked to a learning objective for the whole group, and also to an individual learning target for any child who has learning difficulties.

OFSTED

Defining a set of Early Learning Goals that most children will have attained by the end of their Foundation Stage (the end of their Reception year) has helped to ensure that nursery education is of good quality and provides a sound preparation for later schooling. In order to ensure that the standard of nursery education is consistently high, early years providers registered with their local Early Years Development and Childcare Partnership have to have their educational provision inspected regularly. The nursery inspectors, appointed by the Office for Standards in Education (OFSTED), assess the quality of the early years educational provision and look at the clarity of roles and responsibilities within the setting. They are also interested in plans for meeting the needs of individual children (including those with special educational needs) and developing improved partnerships with parents and carers.

The Scottish framework

In Scotland, there is also a curriculum framework for three- to five-year-olds. There are five key aspects of learning: Emotional, personal and social development (including religious and moral development); Knowledge and understanding of the world (including environmental studies and mathematics); Communication and language; Expressive and aesthetic development, and Physical development and movement. The activities suggested in this book will also be relevant to these Areas of Learning.

The need for individual education plans

One characteristic of Early Years Action for the child with SEN is the writing of an individual education plan or IEP. This is a plan outlines ways for the child to progress. An example of an IEP follows, with a photocopiable proforma on the photocopiable sheet on page 85. This plan should be reviewed regularly with the carers and should be seen as an integrated aspect of the curriculum planning for the whole group. It should only include that which is additional to or different from the differentiated early years curriculum that is in place for all the children.

Case Study: Holly

Holly is now four years old. She is a cheerful, sociable little girl who enjoys early learning and play, and whose development has been assessed by her local Child Development Centre as being around one year behind in all areas. Her family is keen to see her take her place in their local school nursery where her brother and sister went before her. She is well known in the community, and has a lot of friends. Her parents hope that being with other children with good language skills will help Holly to build up her own language which is still very unclear and comes in short phrases. She sees a speech and language therapist once a week at the Health Centre, and, until she started at nursery, was on the Portage home teaching scheme. A Portage worker would call round to her home once a week, negotiate with her parents what should be the next step in her development and how this should be taught. She made such good progress that it was felt that she would manage at her local nursery without any additional support at this stage.

However, it was suggested that the nursery review her progress carefully, and perhaps move towards a statutory assessment of her needs if she seemed to need further support or resourcing. Her needs are therefore being monitored through planning Early Years Action Plus, with outside advice from the Early Years Support Teacher. Her nursery school draws up an individual education plan at least every term, and meets with her parents and outside professionals regularly to review it.

Working with parents and carers

Parents and carers often ask how they can help at home when areas of concern are expressed by the early years setting. They might also approach staff at their children's setting with concerns of their own that they would like to address with them. Parents and carers are the primary educators of their children and should be included as an essential part of the whole-group approach to meeting a child's needs from the start. They have expert knowledge on their own children, and early years providers should aim to create an ethos which shows how much this information is valued and made use of. Information sharing is important and is a two-way process.

There are various practical ways of involving parents and carers in meeting their children's needs:

● Make a personal invitation to parents and carers. For various reasons, they do not always call into the setting on a daily basis. It is helpful to invite them into the setting to share information about their children's achievements in an informal way, or to arrange a home visit if possible.

Individual education plan

Name: Holly Smith | **Early Years Action Plus** | 13

Nature of difficulty: Holly's development is still immature and is about a year behind her age, according to the Child Development Centre. Holly has Down's syndrome.

Action

1 Seeking further information
Elaine will ask the Child Development Centre for further information and find out if any other professionals are involved. In particular, we will ask whether the speech and language therapist can call to see Holly in nursery and share a programme with the staff for encouraging her language and understanding. We will also ask to see the Portage assessment profile, to find out what Holly has already learned and to plan activities to generalize these skills in nursery.

2 Seeking training
We would like to learn more about teaching Holly to develop step by small step. Susan will approach the Portage Service and enquire about courses.

3 Assessing Holly
We need a system of monitoring and recording which fits in with our nursery activities. Marie will send for some developmental and play checklists for us to select a useful system.

Help from parents
● Jane and Brian Smith agree to make a point of talking with Holly's key worker, Elaine, every Friday after nursery.
● A home–setting diary will go between nursery and home, to be completed at each end.
● Every Monday, Holly will bring in a favourite toy or item of interest to share with the other children at circle time.

Targets for this term
● Holly will play for five minutes in the home corner with another child and manage a simple conversation.
● Holly will look and listen to the adult leader in music time with reminders 50% of the time.
● Holly will use coloured crayons to copy a circular scribble and a horizontal and a vertical line.
● Holly will learn to take off her jacket, hang it on a peg, and also pour her own drink.
● Holly will learn to take turns with two other children on the slide.

Review meeting with parents: In six weeks' time. Invite the Early Years Support Teacher, Portage worker and speech and language therapist as well as parents, staff and SENCO for our school.

● Draw their attention to a specific display, where examples of their children's work can be seen.

● Show parents and carers what their children have already achieved and cite examples of progress in their learning made within your setting. At the same time, do not make them feel too despondent if there have not been improvements at home. Use the 'good news' as a hope for positive changes to come.

● Ask the children to show their parents or carers what they can do, what they can say, or what they have learned.

● Ask parents and carers for their opinions, by allowing opportunities for them to contribute information and share experiences. It is often helpful to set a regular time aside when other demands will not intrude.

● Thank parents and carers regularly for their support.

● Celebrate success with parents and carers. This will ensure an ongoing positive partnership.

● Use a home–setting diary to keep in touch. A two-way system of sharing information about a child's success, experiences and opportunities can help in supporting the child.

Working with outside agencies

When assessing and working with a young child who has SEN, an outside professional might be involved in helping the setting to monitor and meet the child's needs. For children with learning difficulties, this is likely to be an Early Years Support Teacher or members of the local Child Development Team. The kind of advice and support available will vary with local policies and practices.

A Portage home visitor might be involved in helping the child to learn new steps in their development. It is helpful to meet with the parents or carers and the Portage worker so that you can learn about the approaches which have been helpful to the child, see the Portage Assessment checklist and use this as a starting-point for your own teaching and monitoring in your setting.

Sometimes, you will be identifying a child's learning difficulties for the first time and you may reach the stage where you feel that outside professional help is needed. Usually, a request for help from outside agencies is likely to follow a decision taken by the SENCO, colleagues and carers when reviewing a child's progress in the setting, asking questions such as, 'Has progress been made?', 'What do carers feel?', 'Do we need more information and advice on the child's needs from outside?' and so on.

Developing inclusive practice

'Inclusion' is the practice of including all children together in a setting. All children participate fully in the regular routines and activities of the classroom or playroom, though these might need to be modified to meet individual children's goals and objectives. This is why the activities in this book carry both learning objectives for *all* the children (with and without SEN) and individual targets for the child who has SEN.

What factors support inclusive practices? Ideas for promoting inclusion for children who have learning difficulties are looked at in the next chapter.

HELPING CHILDREN WITH LEARNING DIFFICULTIES

This chapter explores what is meant by 'learning difficulties' and provides practical suggestions for making the early years curriculum more accessible for these children.

The conditions covered

The ideas in this book are targeted mainly at children who have a general delay in their development and learning. Sometimes, you may hear these difficulties described as 'cognitive difficulties' or 'general learning difficulties'. But it is rarely a 'black and white' issue as to whether or not a child has learning difficulties.

This is why it makes more sense to consider a child's learning in the context of a wide continuum covering how *all* children learn and develop. Some children achieve their developmental milestones ahead of most other children their age. Some children achieve their milestones later than others. Somewhere along this continuum, we might decide

that a child is learning and progressing more slowly than their peers and that we should adopt special approaches to encourage their progress. The *Code of Practice* for special educational needs introduced in Chapter 1 and described more fully in the series handbook helps you to set a child's learning difficulties into a wider context and to plan a graduated approach to meeting their needs. Very approximately, one fifth of all children may be expected to have some kind of learning difficulty, general or otherwise, at some stage of their educational careers.

Down's syndrome

In a few children it is obvious that there are risks of general learning difficulties from birth. For example, children with Down's syndrome usually have a greater difficulty learning than the majority of children their age. The word 'syndrome' means a collection of signs and characteristics. All people with Down's syndrome have certain facial and other physical characteristics which make them appear similar. However, it is important to realize that there are far more differences between people with Down's syndrome than similarities. Each child is an individual in his or her own right and we need to respect this. One baby in about 1,000 is born with Down's syndrome. It is caused by a third twenty-first chromosome in each body cell, so people with Down's syndrome have 47 chromosomes instead of the usual 46. This results in the development of the growing baby in the womb becoming disrupted and altered.

The chances of a baby being born with Down's syndrome increases with the mother's age, particularly when she is over the age of 35.

This is one of the reasons why older mothers are screened during pregnancy. Many children with Down's syndrome are healthy but 40 per cent have heart problems at birth and some might need surgery. There is also a much higher risk of hearing difficulties, vision needs careful monitoring and there is a tendency towards more frequent infections and 'chestiness' too.

Profound learning difficulties

For some of the children who have general learning difficulties, there might have been a cause very early in pregnancy or soon after birth. Perhaps there was some damage to the developing brain, or perhaps the conditions in the womb were not ideal because of other factors. Sometimes children affected in this way can have profound and multiple learning difficulties in which all of their senses and abilities remain at an early stage of development. I have included a few activities in this book that are particularly useful for including this group of children.

Causes

There are a few medical conditions to do with the body chemistry which can contribute to learning difficulties. Some early childhood illnesses, if serious enough, can also leave a child with developmental delay.

However, for most children identified as having general learning difficulties, there will be no known cause. Perhaps they have not yet had all the opportunities that they need to feel stimulated and to learn. Perhaps their self-esteem is very low and they lack the confidence to learn. Perhaps they seem to need more time than other children to acquire new learning. It does not matter what may have caused the delay in the past. Your task in the setting is to identify the fact that a child might be learning more slowly than his or her peers and to provide all the right opportunities and support to bring that child on. This is an exciting challenge and, with careful planning, you should have the pleasure of celebrating success, step by small step.

Addressing needs

This step-by-step approach is central to helping children who have learning difficulties. Your task is not to 'cure' a learning difficulty as if it were a medical condition; it is to identify the difficulty and to plan the appropriate support, either within your setting or with the help of outside agencies. If you start to think in terms of planning and celebrating progress rather than 'curing', then you, the child and the parents or carers will all come to feel much more positive about how your teaching is progressing.

Sometimes you will find that the very fact that you have identified a 'gap' in a child's knowledge and understanding and that you have planned an approach to help will mean that the gap no longer exists. Suddenly, the child will be doing all the same early learning activities which most other children their age are doing. That child no longer has a 'learning difficulty'.

In other cases, you will find that the child will always have a need for specially planned and supported activities, and you will continue to 'differentiate' the curriculum that you are offering them. Do not hold back from thinking in terms of 'special needs' if your input is going to make a real difference. The fact that you are putting into place special approaches does not 'label' the child and create a problem; it helps to prevent a problem from being there. It is for this reason that we are asked to view the *Code of Practice* as a flexible aid, adopting it from time to time with children who might have a real need at any one time for that little bit extra in terms of careful planning and input.

If we provide a differentiated and flexible early years curriculum, then we can truly hope to include all children's needs within our settings. Differentiation is addressed in more detail later in this chapter, along with reflection on what it means to be inclusive. You might also find the section on Portage useful since it is a practical example of step-by-step teaching and partnership with parents and carers.

What you might observe

Nowadays, settings registered with the Early Years Childcare and Development Partnerships are subject to regular inspection and are already familiar with the process of regular monitoring and planning for all their children. The best way of identifying any children who are progressing more slowly than their peers is for this awareness to arise out of your record-keeping and ongoing assessment for *all* the children. You will find ideas for this in the series *Learning in the Early Years* (Scholastic) and, in particular, its series handbook *Ready for Inspection* (see page 96).

What you will be observing, therefore, is not so much a *condition* or a *syndrome* or certain *signs,* so much as the fact that a particular child is not making the progress you might hope for in your setting, given their age and the fact that they have had time to settle with you. This makes the whole process a pragmatic one that relies on common sense, rather than being one that relies on specialist knowledge of 'special conditions'. You already have an expertise in how young children learn and in the curriculum you are delivering to all the children. Your task becomes one of making it accessible to all of them.

Later in this chapter, we will look at two areas in which you can set out to achieve this by making sure that the curriculum you offer is both *inclusive* and *differentiated*.

Educational implications

If you think that a child in your setting has general learning difficulties, what does this mean for your practice? First of all, you will need to find a system of assessment which suits your particular situation. This is so that you can gather evidence of a child's strengths and weaknesses in order to plan suitable approaches. 'Assessment' does not take place in a vacuum, it is an integral part of identifying need, planning for need, making an intervention and evaluating the outcome.

You will read more about assessment in the series handbook. You might decide to observe the child at play and keep objective notes about what their interests are, how they are playing and the language they are using and responding to. There is a very useful training package called 'Quality Play' by Mollie White and John Parry published by the National Portage Association. This training helps you to observe children at play, note the 'starting-points' in their learning and plan special opportunities for encouraging next steps, monitoring their progress carefully and reflectively.

In other settings, colleagues consider what it is that they are hoping to offer in their early years curriculum and then break this down into steps (much smaller than even the QCA Stepping Stones) to form their own assessment schedule for any child with learning difficulties. Here is an example of this kind of thinking.

Example of part of a Curriculum Profile Map
Area of Learning: Personal, social and emotional development

Setting out
- Looks around from parent's knee.
- Reaches out for offered toy.
- Is happy to come into setting with carer.

Stepping Stones 1
- Shows curiosity.
- Has a strong exploratory impulse.
- Has a positive approach to new experiences.

Stepping Stones 2
- Shows increasing independence in selecting and carrying out activities.
- Shows confidence in linking up with others for support and guidance.

Stepping Stones 3
- Displays high levels of involvement in activities.
- Persists for extended periods of time at an activity of his/her choosing.
- Takes risks and explores within the environment.

Early Learning Goal
- Continues to be interested, excited and motivated to learn.
- Is confident to try new activities, initiate ideas and speak in a familiar group.
- Maintains attention, concentration, and sits quietly when appropriate.

Using a checklist

You might decide to use a checklist of play to observe what level the child with special educational needs has reached in their play. This information can then be used as you play alongside the child to encourage and extend their learning and play. The *Playladders* checklist (see page 96) is one example of this.

This developmental checklist is based not on specific areas of development, but on the early years activities themselves. It refers to what is known about the typical ways in which children develop their play when playing with water, when learning to climb, when painting or gluing, or when pretending. The checklist draws together the milestones from existing developmental checklists, and divides these into areas of practical activity. Therefore it should be accessible to an early years educator who does not have the time or resources to withdraw the child for individual assessment. Moreover, the teaching targets that it suggests should make more practical sense for use with the whole class or group.

When using the *Playladders*, early years educators are encouraged to play alongside the child as part of their regular activities within a group of children. By observing how the child is playing, it becomes easy to visualize and record the stage on the *Playladders* later, once all the children have gone home. Play thus proceeds uninterrupted by the assessment and recording.

Once the play behaviour is recorded on the checklist, a 'next step on the ladder' is suggested, and this new skill can be encouraged or taught at a future play session. This is helpful towards providing activities at a level appropriate to the child, or adapting an existing activity so that the child is always included.

Differentiation

Once you have assessed a child's pattern of strengths and weaknesses, thereby establishing the 'starting-point' for your teaching, you will need to differentiate your teaching so that each step will be achievable by the child who has learning difficulties. There follow various examples of ways that you can do this.

Content

For example, the content of a story will need to be at a level appropriate to the child's stage of language. You might need to include concrete props to hold attention, emphasize meaning and allow a child to participate with more than one sense at once. The activity chapters offer examples of ways to do this.

Pace

Allow the child extra time to respond, or ensure that you sometimes give them opportunities to 'get there first'. In this way you will build up their confidence. Activities may need to be presented at a slower pace to ensure understanding, or a succession of materials presented to maintain interest during a discussion. Some children need to sandwich short periods of structured activity with periods of free-play or quiet time. Some children take a long time to process information, and need longer silences than usual if they are to answer a question or fulfil a request. Others may find it hard to remember more than the last piece of information given to them, and therefore need supporting and prompting at each step, taking longer to carry out structured activities. Again, the 'Special support' sections of the activities will prompt you to do many of these things.

Level

When you are planning your curriculum leading towards the Early Learning Goals, you are bound to be making allowances for different levels of ability. Within this, some children might need the learning steps broken down further, and it may be necessary to give value to a smaller and less obvious learning outcome or Stepping Stone. You have read one example of how this might be done in the area of Personal, social and emotional development (see page 19). Further information on breaking teaching steps down (or 'task analysis') can be found in the series handbook.

Access

This involves the way in which materials and resources are presented. Some children may need adapted scissors to cut out a picture (see page 96), or require photographs rather than line drawings in order to name objects. Pictures and illustrations might need to be simplified to cut down on additional and confusing information. Some children might need toys and playthings which are chunky and easy to handle (such as simple jigsaws with knobs on the pieces). Others might need table-tops at a suitable height for them to access when in a standing frame. Some might need radio hearing aids to hear, or to sit close to large picture books to see. The activities in this book often prompt you to take up this kind of thinking.

Response

Some children may be able to show that they have learned through actions rather than words and any response that the child is able to give needs to be valued. For example, some rely on sign language to make

their sounds clear; others may not be able to tell you their wishes, but can demonstrate by their smiles or their choices where they would like to play.

Sequence

Some children need to have opportunities provided at different times, or need to cover different aspects of a topic at separate sessions. If attention is short, it might be necessary to revisit an activity at another time in order to ensure success. Some children find it harder to settle and to concentrate after they have been very active. Others need to 'let off steam' for a while in order to return more attentively to an activity.

Structure

Some children learn best when they are playing in a highly structured setting and are being led and supported by an adult. Others seem to respond best when provided with free play and supported in developing their own agendas. Every child needs opportunities to play and to learn both on their own terms and in groups with other adults and children.

Teacher time

Some children need more individual adult support and time. This can include some one-to-one work or withdrawal into a small group, but mainly refers to supporting the child with additional encouragement and prompting within the regular group. Simply having a heightened awareness of the child's individual needs can affect teacher involvement. In an inclusive setting, any time spent relating individually to an adult would take place in the nursery room itself, with opportunities for involving other children as well.

Grouping

The group structure may afford opportunities to allow the child to respond or for other members of the group to provide good models which can reinforce the child's learning. Sometimes meeting the needs

of individual children with special educational needs has led to children working alone on individual materials. This is not providing the child with an inclusive curriculum. Arrangements to include the child's individual education plan within planning for the whole group can overcome this and lead to a more purposeful and supportive way of meeting special needs. You will read more about how to include your individual planning for the child within your medium- and long-term planning for the whole group in the series handbook.

Differentiated teaching

All of these approaches to differentiation are common sense and arise from personal knowledge and experience of the child and their particular needs. Taking time in the early stages to closely observe and monitor the child can help you to 'tune in' to the way in which they are experiencing their session, allowing for more practical differentiation where opportunities are lacking.

Once you have decided where you are starting from in your teaching (assessment) and have planned a differentiated teaching approach (intervention), then you will need to carefully monitor the child's progress and share this with the parents or carers, continually reviewing how you are all doing and where to go next. You will find more ideas about this in the series handbook.

Looking for inclusive opportunities

There seem to be certain common features that promote inclusion:
● There is usually careful joint planning. For example, if there is special support for a child, how will it be used? Will the child still have access to the full range of adults, children and activities?

● Staff use of educational labels rather than categories or medical labels (such as 'learning difficulty' rather than 'educationally subnormal' or 'mentally handicapped', or even 'child who has SEN' rather than 'SEN child').

● Teachers and adults provide good role models for the children because of their positive expectations and the way they respect and value the children.

● Special attention is given to improving the children's language and communication skills.

● Teaching strategies are developed which enable *all* the children to participate and to learn.

● Individual approaches are planned which draw on pupils' earlier experiences, set high expectations, and encourage mutual peer support.

● There is a flexible use of support aimed at promoting joining in and inclusion rather than at creating barriers and exclusion.

It is hoped that the activities that are provided in this book will help early years practitioners to move towards meeting these conditions for the promotion of inclusion. The publications by Judy Sebba and Darshan Sachdev, and by Mary Dickins provide further information (see page 96).

How inclusive is your setting's policy?

● Do you make it clear that your setting is inclusive and that it welcomes all children, whatever their individual needs?

● Is this clearly stated in any parents' and carers' handbooks?

● Does your setting meet the requirements of the SEN *Code of Practice*?

● Do staff members have the opportunities to take up training in both special needs and early years practice?

● Is your curriculum planning suitable for all children? Are there opportunities for all children to have positive outcomes from each learning opportunity that you plan?

● Do you share observations and planning with parents and carers on a regular basis?

● Do you use methods of communication that include everyone and that can be used between the children, and between the children and your staff (such as including sign language and using more than one language within your setting)?

● Are you prepared to be flexible and change what you are doing in order to meet a particular child's needs?

● Are you happy to involve professionals from outside agencies and to include them in your planning?

- Will all your staff work and plan together to meet any special educational needs?
- Can you provide families with the names and contact details of relevant support services?

Home teaching programmes

In certain situations, early years professionals might find themselves working alongside, or following on from, a Portage home visiting service. Portage was first introduced to this country in the late 1970s at a time when parents and carers would have traditionally been taking their children along to a child development centre for assessment, therapy and 'expert advice'. Parents and carers found themselves having to relate to many different professionals, while their own expertise and in-depth knowledge of their children were not being harnessed to the full.

There are now Portage home teaching services throughout the UK and beyond. Registration and training are co-ordinated by the National Portage Association (see page 96). Many services were set up with Education Support Grant funding, with the idea that local agencies (most often the LEA) would take on the longer-term funding. During Portage, there is a regular, generally weekly, visit to the home by a trained home visitor. A shared assessment framework, usually the Portage checklist, is used which draws on the child's development to establish a profile of strengths and needs. There is a programme of teaching activities tailored to the needs of the individual child. There follows positive monitoring of the child's progress with regular review. Management and advisory support for the service is provided by a team composed of representatives from all the contributing agencies and the parents or carers.

Sometimes, a child with learning difficulties might have been receiving Portage home teaching before joining your setting. Ask the parents or carers to share the Portage checklist with you so that you can celebrate the progress already achieved by the child and continue to teach them. In order to do this, you will need to have in your mind clear information about what the child can do *now* and a clear idea of what you wish the child to be able to do in the *future* – your long-term goal. You then need to break the teaching task down into small manageable steps so that the child whom you are targeting will succeed, in small steps. This process is called 'task analysis' and is explained more fully in the series handbook.

There are many other schemes that have developed to support and strengthen the role of parents and carers in educating their young children. One set of materials aimed at families of younger pre-school children is the *Playsense* pack (see page 96).

PERSONAL, SOCIAL AND EMOTIONAL DEVELOPMENT

In this chapter you will find ideas for supporting children with learning difficulties, including encouraging confidence, helping them to settle in, and breaking skills down into easier stages.

LEARNING OBJECTIVES FOR ALL THE CHILDREN
● to be confident to speak in a familiar group
● to form good relationships with adults and peers.

INDIVIDUAL LEARNING TARGET
● to sign a greeting and give eye contact.

Welcome signs

Group size
All the children.

What to do
This activity could form the first or final activity in a session. Sit with the children in a circle and teach them the welcome song below, to a simple tune, such as 'For He's a Jolly Good Fellow'.

> Good morning, children! Good morning, children!
> Good morning, children! And how are you today?

Good   **Morning**

Introduce the Makaton sign for 'Good morning' as you sing: make a thumbs up sign for 'good', followed by your fist 'drawing the curtains open' across your body (see left).

Once the children are familiar with the song, move around the inside of the circle, signing and singing the song to each child. Crouch down to their level and use a light touch if you need to in order to encourage eye contact and a smile. Encourage them to give the thumbs up sign for 'good' in reply.

Special support
This activity is useful for including a child for whom Makaton sign language has been recommended. Makaton is helpful because it encourages children with learning, hearing or language difficulties to speak as well as to sign, and it makes what they are saying easier to interpret and respond to (see page 96 for a useful address). Spend one-to-one time with the children that you are targeting to practise the sign for 'good'. Use hand-over-hand support at first if you need to.

Extension
Introduce the Makaton signs for 'How are you?' (see right).

LINKS WITH HOME
Find out about any signs that the children use with their parents or carers so that you can continue their use in the setting.

How are you?

LEARNING OBJECTIVE FOR ALL THE CHILDREN
● to be interested, excited and motivated to learn.

INDIVIDUAL LEARNING TARGET
● to have a short go at each nursery activity and to know what is on offer there.

Having a go

Group size
Individual SEN child within whole group.

What you need
An assessment system such as the *Playladders* booklet (see page 96); the photocopiable sheet on page 86; the Stepping Stones from the early years curriculum, or design your own system using the sheet.

What to do
You will already have your own way of monitoring and assessing each child's progress within your group. If you need help here, you might find the Scholastic series *Learning in the Early Years* useful (see page 96). Appoint key workers to observe, play alongside and assess how each child is playing at regular intervals.

Special support
You will need to assess and monitor the progress of a child with learning difficulties in more detail than for the other children. Spend time setting up different areas so that you can see how the child is playing in each of them: in the water tray, with the sand, in the home corner and outside. Note down how they play when they are unsupported, then play alongside them and record how they play when an adult is encouraging and extending their play. This gives you a more dynamic way of assessing how the child is playing and learning.

Use a copy of the photocopiable sheet on page 86 each half-term to record how the individual child is playing and how you plan to develop this over the next half-term. Your planning should fit neatly with the individual education plan for the child (see the photocopiable sheet on page 85) and with your medium-term planning for the whole group. Make a note of how the child plays with each activity at the moment, how you would like to encourage them to play with this activity over the next few weeks and ways that you will implement this. Make sure that you build in a review time so that you have the opportunity to think about how this went, leading neatly into your next series of planning sheets.

Extension
Always have in mind the 'next steps' for the child in any activity so that you can be constantly extending and encouraging their play.

LINKS WITH HOME
Share the progress that you have recorded with parents and carers at regular intervals.

LEARNING OBJECTIVE FOR ALL THE CHILDREN
● to work together harmoniously.

INDIVIDUAL LEARNING TARGET
● to play co-operatively with a partner.

Rainbow game

Group size
Eight to 12 children.

What you need
Silk, chiffon scarves or sari material in a range of colours, at least one for each pair of children; gentle music, such as Ravel's *Bolero*, on CD or tape; CD or tape recorder.

What to do
Gather the children together and sit in a circle on the floor. Toss the fabrics into the centre of the circle and invite the children to feel and explore the colours and textures. Talk about the wonderful colours and how the fabric feels. Encourage the children to gently raise scarves in the air and watch them fall again.

Make sure that each child has a scarf, then stand up together. Encourage the children to watch you and copy your movements. Play the music and gently wave your scarf around, making circles, making it float high and low and drawing it across your face. Now invite a child to be the leader if they would like to, and encourage everyone to copy them.

Finally, invite the children to sit down opposite each other in pairs, holding their two scarves between them, one in each hand. Show them a gentle rocking 'dance' for which they hold their scarves high and rock gently from side to side. Admire the beautiful rainbow effect you are creating as the scarves gently rock and flow.

Special support
Make sure that the child whom you are targeting has a chance to be leader in the first part of the activity. Support him or her in thinking of ideas for the other children to copy. In the second part of the activity, support the child as he or she works with a partner, instead of partnering them yourself.

Extension
Encourage older children to invent rainbow dances and teach them to you.

LINKS WITH HOME
Invite parents and carers to bring in fabrics and clothing from a range of cultures to admire and talk about together.

LEARNING OBJECTIVES FOR ALL THE CHILDREN
● to dress and undress independently
● to have a developing respect for their own culture and appearance and those of others.

INDIVIDUAL LEARNING TARGET
● to gradually improve dressing and undressing skills.

LINKS WITH HOME
Use the home–setting diary to keep in touch with how the child that you are targeting is progressing in independence skills, and what methods of teaching seem to be helpful.

Changing room

Group size
All the children at various times.

What you need
A selection of dressing-up clothes such as hats, scarves, shoes, gloves, and so on; standard mirror which is safe for child use; if possible, shelves and low rails.

What to do
Arrange the clothing on low rails and on shelves (improvise using cardboard boxes on their sides if you do not have these) to look like a department store. Spread the clothes out so that they can be easily seen and are attractive. Set up the mirror where the children can admire themselves. Play alongside them to begin the game. Imagine that you are shopping in a department store and buying new clothes. Be on hand to help the children put on the clothes and assist with fastenings, using this as a natural opportunity for showing them how to manage themselves.

Special support
This is an ideal opportunity to teach dressing and undressing skills. Play alongside the child that you are targeting and use various items of clothing to see how much they can do all by themselves and how much help you need to give.

Decide upon a reasonable 'next step' for the child. Perhaps you would like to teach them to pull on socks. Work out a series of steps involved, such as placing the sock onto the toes, pulling the sock up to the heel, pulling the sock over the heel and then pulling the sock up. Choose the step that is the easiest, probably the last, and help the children with the others, allowing them to complete this one on their own. Praise and celebrate their success. This method of teaching is called 'backwards chaining' because you are teaching the child progressively backwards through the various steps of the task. You will be able to find other dressing skills where this method would be very helpful.

Extension
Provide a mannequin on which the children can design whole outfits.

LEARNING OBJECTIVES FOR ALL THE CHILDREN
● to be confident to try new activities within a familiar group
● to form good relationships with peers.

INDIVIDUAL LEARNING TARGET
● to look, listen and remember two pieces of information.

Remember me!

Group size
Six children.

What to do
Sit together in a circle on the floor. Use this activity when you have children who have recently joined the setting and when you are helping the children to remember new names.

Tell the children that you are going to play a game based on their names. Go around the circle asking the children to say their names. If a child is very shy, simply say it for them and move on.

Now ask each child to think of an action to go with their name. Start by saying your own name and, for example, patting your head at the same time. Encourage each child to think of an action that is different from everyone else's. Again, speak and act for any child who is feeling shy.

Go to each child in turn and ask the rest of the group to see if they can remember the child's name and the action that they did. Ask the child concerned if you are right. Continue until the group has remembered everyone's action.

Finally, suggest an action and ask the group to remember which child chose it. Who clapped their hands? Who stamped their foot? Praise all the children for remembering well.

Special support
Make sure that the child whom you are targeting has one of the first turns to choose an action to make it easier for them. Start in a smaller group of three or four if you need to.

Extension
Invite older children to choose and carry out an action word that starts with the same letter as their name, such as, 'I'm Suki and I'm singing!'.

LINKS WITH HOME
Encourage the children to introduce their friends to their parents or carers at home time, remembering their names.

LEARNING OBJECTIVE FOR ALL THE CHILDREN
● to maintain attention, concentrate and sit quietly when appropriate.

INDIVIDUAL LEARNING TARGET
● to listen quietly and look towards a sound.

Quiet as a mouse

Group size
Ten to sixteen children.

What you need
A selection of percussion instruments (such as shakers, tambourines and bells) in a box.

What to do
Sit together in a circle. You can use this activity as part of your regular music time or circle time. Choose one of the instruments from your box and make a sound with it. Pass it around the circle and ask each child to make their own sound with it. Ask the children to pass the instrument around again, but this time to try to pass it silently. Shut your eyes as you pretend not to hear where the instrument has reached in the circle. Invite the children to take turns to sit in the centre of the circle with their eyes closed and pointing with their fingers if they hear the instrument make a sound. Next, pass an instrument around asking each child to make as loud a noise as possible with it.

Pass the box of instruments around and ask each child to choose one. Encourage them to copy you as you play very loudly and then very quietly. Invite them to stand up and march in a line, again copying the leader's volume.

Return to your circle and pass the box around, inviting each child to place their instrument into it without making any noise. Make sure that you praise their efforts.

Special support
Emphasize the key words 'loudly' and 'quietly', as you play. Sit beside the child that you are targeting so that you can focus their attention when they are listening for sounds and when they are handling the instrument silently.

Extension
Introduce hand signals to indicate 'loud' or 'quiet' when you are all playing your instruments in a circle.

LINKS WITH HOME
Explain to parents and carers that you have been working on being gentle and quiet. Suggest that they show their children how to close a door as quietly as possible.

Showing off

Group size
Six children.

What you need
A camera; film.

What to do
Carry out the background work for this activity over three or four weeks. Look for activities that each child is particularly enjoying and take a photograph of it. Take care not to celebrate only the finished products – record the process too. You can also use these photographs as part of your evidence of the children's progress and your general record-keeping.

When the photographs are developed, make a selection that includes each child. Sit with the group and talk about the pictures. Encourage the children to remember what they were doing and tell you why they were enjoying it. Ask them, 'Who is in the photograph?', 'Where are you?', 'What are you doing?', 'What happened next?' and so on.

Invite the children to choose one photograph each to show and talk about at circle time. When each child is ready, gather in a circle and take it in turns to pass the photograph around as you ask questions about it. Encourage the whole group to join in the discussion.

Special support
Keep your questioning very simple, at first asking questions which require only a 'yes' or 'no' response, for example, 'Is this you?', 'Is that your model?', 'Did you do it all by yourself?' and so on. Support and encourage the child as he or she talks in front of the group.

Extension
Mount the photographs in a book and ask the children to dictate or write labels for each photograph.

LEARNING OBJECTIVE FOR ALL THE CHILDREN
● to be confident to speak in a familiar group.

INDIVIDUAL LEARNING TARGET
● to answer a simple 'yes' or 'no' question in front of a familiar group.

LINKS WITH HOME
Encourage the children to show their photographs to parents and carers and answer their questions about them.

LEARNING OBJECTIVE FOR ALL THE CHILDREN
● to have a developing awareness of their own feelings and those of others.

INDIVIDUAL LEARNING TARGET
● to match and name different expressions and feelings.

Feeling Lotto

Group size
Four children.

What you need
Eight copies of the photocopiable sheet on page 87; eight sheets of A4 card; glue; scissors.

What to do
Stick each photocopy firmly onto card. Cut four of them up into six separate emotion cards. Sit together around a table and give each child an uncut sheet. Talk about the faces and ask questions such as, 'Which one looks sad?', 'What is this one feeling?', 'Do you think that one is bored?', and so on. Share the four packs of cards out, one for each child.

Mix up the 24 cards and place them face down in the middle of the table. Help the children to take it in turns to choose a card and match it to an expression on their sheet. If the correct square is already covered by a card, they should offer it to a child who still needs it. In this way, everyone 'wins'. Encourage polite requests, saying 'please' and 'thank you'. Name the expressions together as you match them. Talk about things that make the children cross, sad, happy and so on.

Special support
Start this activity with just one child working with the child that you are targeting. You can make the matching easier by adding some background colour to the faces on the sheets and the cards; perhaps yellow for all the 'happy' faces, blue for 'sad', red for 'cross' and so on.

Extension
Use the cards to play 'Pairs' or 'Snap!'.

LINKS WITH HOME
Explain to parents and carers that you have been doing some work on feelings. It would be helpful if they could assist their children with finding words for their feelings when they are particularly upset or happy.

LEARNING OBJECTIVES FOR ALL THE CHILDREN
● to form good relationships with peers
● to work together harmoniously.

INDIVIDUAL LEARNING TARGET
● to be involved and co-operate in play with a partner.

Side by side

Group size
Two children at a time.

What you need
Slide; safety mat; play tunnel; teddy bear; bubble-making kit.

What to do
These activities are helpful for a child who is at the very earliest stages of watching other children and joining in. Set up the slide and the tunnel and stay close to the child that you are targeting as you watch and talk about how the children are playing. At this stage, you are simply encouraging them to look.

As the child begins to want to play, continue to point out what the other children are doing so that you can make them aware of turn-taking and where the other children are.

Choose a partner for the child that you are targeting to play with. Encourage the partner to take the teddy up to the top of the slide and push him down. Encourage the child that you are targeting to retrieve the teddy at the bottom and then to push the teddy down the slide. The partner can then pick the teddy up and a simple turn-taking game will have developed.

Let the children move to the tunnel and invite one child to call 'Hello!' as their partner's face appears at the other end. Encourage a turn-taking 'Hello!' game for a few minutes.

Finally, introduce the bubbles and encourage the child's partner to blow bubbles for the child to catch and burst. Praise both children for playing together.

Special support
Look for opportunities throughout the session to draw the child's attention to other children, watching, copying and joining in with your support. Keep the groups of children small to begin with.

Extension
Set up a turn-taking game in which the children roll coloured ice cubes down a plastic tube into the water tray for another child to catch before they melt!

LINKS WITH HOME
If you are targeting a child at this early stage, talk with parents and carers about setting up opportunities at home for the child to meet and play with one other child.

LEARNING OBJECTIVE FOR ALL THE CHILDREN
● to form good relationships with peers.

INDIVIDUAL LEARNING TARGET
● to play co-operatively with a partner.

Hat tricks

Group size
Eight children (or adapt for even numbers).

What you need
Eight cards on which you have drawn eight different hats; another set of eight cards with the same hats drawn on; assortment of hats, including dressing-up hats such as firefighters', police and space helmets; musical tape or CD; tape recorder or CD player; teddy or soft toy.

What to do
Invite the children to sit down in a circle and tell them that you are about to play a 'Musical hats' game. Give each child a different hat picture to hold. Place the second set of pictures in one of the hats. Pass the hat around the circle and ask each child to pick out a card. Help each child to identify the child who is holding the same picture and to move so that they are sitting next to each other.

Now place all the real hats in the centre of the circle. Tell the children that they should pass the teddy around the circle while the music is playing. Show them which way the teddy should go. When the music stops, the children should stop passing. Who has the teddy?

Invite that child and their partner to stand up and choose a hat for each other. Enjoy the effect and then return the hats to the floor and continue the game until each pair has had their chance to choose hats.

Special support
Stay close to the child that you are targeting so that you can encourage them to think about their partner and choose a hat for them. Praise them for playing with their partner.

Extension
Ask older children to help you make the picture cards.

LINKS WITH HOME
Think of ways in which the children can play co-operatively with a brother or sister at home, sharing a story at bed-time perhaps. Suggest ideas for making sibling play more harmonious to parents and carers.

COMMUNICATION, LANGUAGE AND LITERACY

These activities provide suggestions for making experiences as concrete as possible for children with learning difficulties and for teaching early communication skills.

LEARNING OBJECTIVES FOR ALL THE CHILDREN
● to communicate clearly
● to interact with others.

INDIVIDUAL LEARNING TARGET
● to use signs, symbols or objects of reference to make their needs known in a range of situations.

My needs

Group size
One targeted child at a time.

What you need
The photocopiable sheet on page 88, laminated.

What to do
When a child whose communication skills are still at an early stage of development joins your setting, it is important to get to know how they make their needs known as quickly as possible. Use the questions on the photocopiable sheet on page 88 as a starting-point and ask the parents or carers to let you know how their child communicates his basic needs or information.

Write down how the child asks for things, shows happiness and unhappiness and how you can tell if the child is frightened. How does the child let you know that they have had enough of something or that they need the toilet or to be changed? What will you be able to see if the child is really interested in something? How do they greet people or say 'goodbye'? Some children might behave in certain ways, some might use gestures, and some might use sounds or words as well. Write these observations down so that you can share the information with colleagues. You might choose to make a laminated card for the child which colleagues can refer to easily. You might make up a personal 'communication book' for that child, adding photographs of the child's different expressions and actions that refer to different emotions.

Special support
Some children benefit from 'objects of reference' to help them to communicate or understand what is coming next. A toy potty can come to indicate 'toilet', a coat can indicate 'home time', a shaker can signal 'music time'. Use objects and actions as well as words in your early stages of communicating with each other.

Extension
Develop this activity for everyone by using it to talk about how we all express our feelings.

LINKS WITH HOME
Review your communication sheet regularly with the parents or carers and make sure that you are up to date with any signs that the child is using at home.

LEARNING OBJECTIVE FOR ALL THE CHILDREN
● to sustain attentive listening, responding to what they have heard by relevant actions.

INDIVIDUAL LEARNING TARGET
● to follow a simple spoken direction.

Drum beats

Group size
Eight to ten children.

What you need
A selection of drums, one for each child (use real drums and beaters, bongo drums, tambours, saucepans and spoons, empty tin boxes and beaters, and upturned plastic buckets and hands).

What to do
Sit together in a circle on the floor. Spread yourselves out to make a larger circle. Arrange the drums in the centre of the circle. Introduce the following chant:

> Drums, drums, the beat of the drums!
> If you walked to school you can play me the drums!

Introduce a new idea for the second line each time you chant it. You might say 'If you're wearing red…' or 'If your name starts with an "s"…' and so on.

Link your requests to the particular topic that you are following or the particular learning skills that you are working on that session. Each time you say the chant, stop to allow the appropriate children to move into the centre of the circle and enjoy a few moments drumming. Let them return to the circle and repeat the chant with a new idea.

Special support
Sit the child that you are targeting next to you so that you can repeat the chant to them quietly, drawing their attention to the key idea. Support them as they work out whether that idea refers to them, and encourage them to move into the drumming centre of the circle at the appropriate times.

Extension
This idea can be extended to include all kinds of early phonic work. You can ask for letters in names, you can give out word cards and ask for children who have certain word sounds and so on.

LINKS WITH HOME
Ask the children to find some form of drum at home and play the game with their parents or carers. It is an excellent way of encouraging children to listen and respond to what their parents or carers are saying in a fun situation.

Changing places

Group size
12 to 24 children.

What to do
Sit in a large circle on the floor. Start by singing the following 'Hello' song to the tune of 'Frère Jacques' so that the children get to know each other's names.

> Hello Charlie, hello Charlie,
> How are you? How are you?
> Very nice to see you! Very nice to see you!
> How d'you do! How d'you do!
>
> *Hannah Mortimer*

Substitute each child's name in the first line. Move around the inside of the circle, making eye contact with each child as you sing and perhaps waving or shaking hands for the first and last lines. Encourage all the children to sing with you and to respond to their names with a smile and a wave.

Play a name game. Take it in turns to ask each child who they would like to say 'hello' to in the circle. If the first child chooses, for example, Jonathan, encourage the child to say, 'Hello Jonathan!' in a loud voice. The first child and Jonathan should then change places. Jonathan now has a turn and changes places with the child of his choice. Continue until every child has had a turn.

Special support
Start by sitting close to any child that you are targeting and allow them to have an early turn. Help them to choose a friend to say 'hello' to by reminding them of some names.

Extension
Challenge the children to 'Say "hello" to someone whose name begins with a "j"' and so on with a different letter for each child.

LEARNING OBJECTIVE FOR ALL THE CHILDREN
● to interact with others, negotiating activities and taking turns in conversation.

INDIVIDUAL LEARNING TARGETS
● to give eye contact when greeted
● to give a simple greeting in return.

LINKS WITH HOME
Send a group photograph home (a snapshot of a small group of children is fine). See if the children can tell their parents or carers the names of the other children in the photograph.

Hello Lily, hello Lily, how are you?

LEARNING OBJECTIVE FOR ALL THE CHILDREN
● to extend their vocabulary, exploring the meanings and sounds of new words.

INDIVIDUAL LEARNING TARGET
● to name a familiar object.

LINKS WITH HOME
Before this activity, suggest two or three object words for parents and carers to teach their children at home. Follow this up by using those objects in your bag.

In the bag

Group size
Ten to 20 children.

What you need
A draw-string bag made of velvet or other attractive fabric; box of small objects such as a toy car, an interesting stone, a fir cone, a folding fan, a small bell, a silver spoon and so on (ensure you have one object for each child).

What to do
Sit on the floor in a circle. Place the box of objects beside you. Reach for one object and hide it in the draw-string bag. Pass the bag around the circle as you sing the song below to the tune of 'Polly Put the Kettle On' (Traditional). Substitute different children's names in the third line and at the end of the verse encourage that child to look inside the bag and tell you what they have found.

> What is in the bag today?
> What is in the bag today?
> Emma's looking in the bag
> To see what's there.
>
> *Hannah Mortimer*

When the object has been identified, substitute a new item and send the bag around the circle again, starting from the first child. Continue until everyone has had a turn.

Special support
When it is the turn of the child that you are targeting, put an object whose name the child is currently learning in the bag.

Extension
Gather a selection of objects related to a particular theme that you are learning about at the moment. You can also make this into a multicultural activity, enjoying and talking about interesting objects from a range of cultures or countries.

LEARNING OBJECTIVES FOR ALL THE CHILDREN
● to interact with others
● to speak clearly and audibly with confidence and control and show awareness of the listener.

INDIVIDUAL LEARNING TARGETS
● to anticipate what is coming next
● to respond socially to another child by smiling and laughing.

LINKS WITH HOME
Encourage parents and carers to play 'peep-bo' games at home with scarves. Can their children pull, or attempt to pull, a scarf off their own face yet?

Peep-bo!

Group size
Four to eight children.

What you need
A light chiffon or silk scarf.

What to do
This is an excellent activity for including any child whose development is still at a very early stage, perhaps because they have profound and multiple learning difficulties.

Sit together informally on a carpet and cushions. Show the children the beautiful scarf and invite them to take turns at covering their faces with it and then pulling it away, saying 'peep-bo!'. Encourage them to look at the child that you are targeting as they pull the scarf away and say 'bo!'. Stay close to encourage the children's play and ensure that everyone is enjoying it.

Now place the scarf lightly over the child that you are targeting. Make sure that they are not distressed and that this remains a mutually enjoyable activity. Invite different children in turn to approach the child and pull away the scarf as you sing the song below to the tune of 'Frère Jacques'.

> Hide Jacob's face! Hide Jacob's face!
> Where is he? Where is he?
> Now we'll try and find him. Now we'll try and find him.
> Here we go… Pe-ep BO!
>
> *Hannah Mortimer*

Encourage the two children to share eye contact and greet each other, joining in with the 'BO'. Praise all the children for being friendly.

Special support
Start with an individual 'Peep-bo' game between you and the child that you are targeting until they come to really enjoy this game. Then introduce this activity with the other children.

Extension
Support the children as they find other ways of including the child that you are targeting in their activities. Communicate for children who cannot speak, telling the other children how much they are enjoying playing with them.

LEARNING OBJECTIVE FOR ALL THE CHILDREN
● to know that print carries meaning.

INDIVIDUAL LEARNING TARGET
● to trace the letters of their name.

Written in clay

Group size
Two or three children.

What you need
Modelling clay; boards; rolling-pins; round-ended potter's utensils for marking the clay (as thick as a child's finger); knife (adult use); aprons; washing-up bowls; towels; paper; wax crayons.

What to do
Set up a washing-up bowl and towels close to the clay so that the children can wash their hands quickly (some children cannot bear the feeling of drying clay on their hands). Put on aprons and enjoy the clay together. Show the children how to handle it and mould it. Demonstrate how they can keep it wet and how they can break pieces off to shape.

Demonstrate to the children how to roll a piece of clay flat on their boards. Aim for about 1cm thickness and provide some final help to make the sheet of clay of uniform thickness. If a child can already write their name, ask them to trace the shape with their finger and then use the utensil to carve out the letters of their name in the clay. Check with the children that the letters are correct. Thank them for their help, use your knife to cut a neat rectangle around the name, and place the 'plaques' on a sunny window sill to dry.

In a subsequent session, encourage the children to trace over the letters of their names with their fingers. Let them place paper over the plaques and take wax crayon rubbings of their names.

Special support
Help the child to trace over the grooves of their name with gentle hand-over-hand support, saying the first letter sound for them.

Extension
Can the children identify their plaques just by feeling?

LINKS WITH HOME
Check with parents and carers that no child has a contact dermatitis affected by clay. If so, you could consider using bread dough as an alternative and then baking it.

Floury patterns

Group size
Two or three children.

What you need
Flour; plastic jug of water; bowl; mixing spoon; food colourings; metal trays (one for each child); aprons; washing-up bowls and towels.

What to do
Enjoy preparing this activity together. Put on your aprons and start by filling the washing-up bowl half-full with flour. Ask one child to add small quantities of water from the jug and another child to mix gently until you have a floppy, fairly runny, consistency. Help a third child to add a few drops of colouring. Take turns to mix it well. Talk about what is happening.

Spoon some of the paste onto each child's tray. It should be just thick enough to make finger marks in it so that the children can enjoy making swirls and line patterns. As the paste flows back, the patterns disappear and a new pattern can be made. Enjoy the feel of this 'messy play' and talk together about what you are all doing.

Finally, encourage each child to write their name with a finger in the paste before it disappears again.

Special support
Invite the child that you are targeting to write just the first letter of their name, saying the letter sound as they write it. Use gentle hand-over-hand help if you need to.

Extension
Make a thicker dough, roll it into balls, decorate them with words and patterns then bake them hard. When they are cool, paint and varnish them and use them as paperweights.

LEARNING OBJECTIVE FOR ALL THE CHILDREN
● to write their own names.

INDIVIDUAL LEARNING TARGET
● to make the initial letter of their name.

LINKS WITH HOME
Suggest this activity for parents and carers to help their children at home. Perhaps they could breathe on a window or mirror and help their children to write the first letter of their name.

COMMUNICATION, LANGUAGE & LITERACY

LEARNING OBJECTIVE FOR ALL THE CHILDREN
● to attempt writing for a variety of purposes.

INDIVIDUAL LEARNING TARGET
● to play with early mark making.

Nursery news!

Group size
All the children.

What you need
A role-play area; paper; pencils; old typewriters; stamps and ink blocks; old newspapers with pictures; the computer; scissors; glue; filing basket; sheets of A3 paper; tape recorder or Dictaphone.

What to do
Set up one corner of the playroom or classroom as a newspaper office. Gather the children together to show them what there is and to talk about newspapers. What are they used for? What do we mean by 'news'? If we wanted to tell people the 'news' about our setting, what information might we give them?

Encourage the children to visit the newspaper office throughout the session, with one helper there at all times to assist. Encourage each child to think of a piece of news, draw a picture of the nursery session, cut something out or dictate a piece of news. Support those children who want to do their own 'typing', mark-making, copying, tracing or writing. Gather the children's contributions together in a filing basket. At the end of the session, assemble the children's contributions by mounting them with glue onto sheets of A3 paper and adding your own commentary to draw the newspaper together. Share it with all the children the next day.

Special support
Make sure that the child whom you are targeting can contribute to the newspaper at whatever level they are currently performing.

Extension
Invite older children to help with the 'production' of the paper, for example, mounting the articles on the A3 paper.

LINKS WITH HOME
Copy your newspaper to send home to parents and carers.

Pairing and sharing

Group size
Two children.

What you need
A camera; collection of about ten familiar objects; card; laminator or sticky-backed plastic; box.

What to do
You will need to plan this activity ahead. Think of about ten familiar objects whose names you are teaching to the child that you are targeting. You might choose a ball, a toy chair, a fork, a spoon, a clock, a brick, a toy car, a doll, a cup and a large button. Take photographs of each one against a plain background. It is important that you have pictures and objects which are identical. In other words, if you have chosen a toy dog as an object, the picture must be of that particular toy dog. Keep your objects all together in a box ready for the activity once the photographs are available.

Mount the ten photographs onto card and laminate them, or coat them with sticky-backed plastic, to make them more durable. Now play a matching game in which the children must pick out a card and match it to one of the real objects in the box.

Special support
Matching pictures to real objects is an important milestone for children with learning difficulties. Start with just three pictures and a choice of three objects. Place the three cards face up on a table and ask the child to place each object on its card. Name the objects as you play. Then increase the choices step by step. Use strong praise and encouragement to keep their attention and to make the task rewarding.

Extension
If you remove one object or one card, can the children remember what is missing?

Just imagine!

Group size
Eight to 12 children.

What you need
A story sack or familiar story with accompanying props, or felt boards and felt story figures.

What to do
Gather the children together and tell them a familiar story, moving the props and making them interact and speak. Then invite different children to be in charge of different props. For example, if you were doing 'The Three Billy Goats Gruff' (Traditional), you might have one child looking after each Billy Goat, one (perhaps shy) child as the Troll, one in charge of the shiny paper which represents the river, and two or three to make and mend the bridge. Retell the story together as the children move the props and speak for the characters of the story. Talk at the end about what might happen next in the story.

Special support
Give the child that you are targeting a repetitive phrase to say, such as 'Who's that trip trapping over my bridge?', or a particularly motivating part to play, such as a roaring Troll, in order to hold their attention. Encourage and support them as they make their prop play its part at the appropriate time.

Extension
Encourage older children to make up their own stories with you and collect props for it.

LEARNING OBJECTIVE FOR ALL THE CHILDREN
● to use language to imagine and re-create roles and experiences.

INDIVIDUAL LEARNING TARGET
● to engage in simple imaginative or symbolic play.

LINKS WITH HOME
Ask the parents or carers of the child that you are targeting for his or her favourite story and try to build the activity around it.

MATHEMATICAL DEVELOPMENT

Children with learning difficulties need their learning experiences to be concrete and practical. In this chapter you will find ideas for keeping the learning steps small and making the activities as rewarding as possible.

Put it in a sock!

Group size
Two or three children.

What you need
Three colourful adult-sized socks; low washing line; pegs; three small teddy bears; self-adhesive stickers; washable felt-tipped pens.

What to do
Hang the washing line up at one end of your room so that it is within the children's height but just in front of a wall so that they do not bump into it.

Peg the three socks in a row. Challenge the children to place one teddy in the first, two teddies in the second, and three teddies in the third. Have the teddies' heads peeping out of the top of the socks if you can. Ask the children to cover their eyes as you rearrange the socks. Can they see how many teddies are in each sock?

Tuck the teddies deep into the socks and rearrange the order. Challenge the children to feel how many teddies are in each sock. Support them as they re-hang the socks in order, from left to right along the line. Encourage each child to write the numbers '1', '2', and '3' on three self-adhesive labels. Help them stick each label onto the right sock.

Special support
Start by giving the child that you are targeting the sock with one teddy in it. Peg up the other socks in order and invite the child to hang up the sock, saying the number out loud. Help them to write a number '1' on their sticker and stick it onto the sock.

Extension
Build up the numbers of socks and teddies to five once the children are familiar with the activity. Hang the socks up in any order and challenge the children to re-peg them in the correct order.

LEARNING OBJECTIVE FOR ALL THE CHILDREN
● to count reliably up to ten everyday objects.

INDIVIDUAL LEARNING TARGET
● to develop one-to-one correspondence to three.

Tally counts

Group size
Four to six children.

What you need
Pieces of card (about 10cm x 10cm); felt-tipped pen; a clipboard and pencil for each child; A4 paper.

What to do
Make up about ten cards in advance. On each one, decide on a set of familiar items in your setting which the children could count easily. There should be no more than ten of any one object, and ideally one of one thing, two of another and so on. For example, you might have one slide, two doors, three windows, four easels and so on until ten children. Draw a little picture of the item on each card and write 'How many... can you count?' (see below).

Clip a sheet of A4 paper onto each clipboard and attach a card at the top. Encourage each child to take a clipboard and show them how they can count the items, making one stroke of their pencil onto the sheet of paper each time they see one of the items in question. Choose cards that are going to be within each child's ability. At first, the children are bound to count items twice, but they will still be practising making one pencil stroke for each item as they count it.

Give each child several turns with different cards. When all the children have finished counting and marking, compare and check your results together.

Special support
Use sets of just one, two and three items until the child that you are targeting is ready to count further.

Extension
Teach older children how to group tally marks into sets of five.

LINKS WITH HOME
Ask the parents or carers of the child that you are targeting to help them count out plates, knives, forks and so on at mealtimes.

LEARNING OBJECTIVE FOR ALL THE CHILDREN
● to use everyday words to describe position.

INDIVIDUAL LEARNING TARGET
● to respond appropriately to 'under' and 'in'.

LINKS WITH HOME
Ask the parents or carers of the child that you are targeting to play a game with their child at bedtime. They could hide the child's favourite cuddly toy in or under the bed, telling their child where to look for it and praising their success.

Hide-and-seek

Group size
Four to six children.

What you need
A little teddy bear and a larger teddy bear; toy bed with legs; bedclothes for the toy bed; small box, large enough to put the little teddy bear in.

What to do
Gather everyone together in a circle. Introduce 'Little Teddy' to the children and show off her beautiful bed and bedclothes and her 'toy box'. Show her playing in her bedroom and then becoming tired. Say 'Here comes Mummy Ted to put her to bed but, oh dear! Teddy is hiding!'. Turn to the first child in the circle and ask him or her to hide Little Ted 'in the box' or 'under the bed'. Show Mummy Ted looking for Little Ted and ask the children to help her by telling her where Little Ted is hiding, for example, 'She's in the box!'.

Develop the story as each child has a turn following your instructions and hiding Little Teddy in a different place. Let the child that you are targeting finish the game by placing Little Ted 'in the bed'. Sing a goodnight song to Little Ted together.

Special support
Spend some time before this activity teaching the child that you are targeting how to put Teddy in or under the bed.

Extension
Sometimes Little Teddy could hide 'behind the box'. This will raise some interesting discussion on which side of the box would be 'behind' so that Mummy Ted could not see Little Teddy!

LEARNING OBJECTIVE FOR ALL THE CHILDREN
● to use language such as 'more' or 'less'.

INDIVIDUAL LEARNING TARGET
● to identify which group of children is 'more'.

LINKS WITH HOME
Ask the parents or carers of the child that you are targeting to find opportunities to encourage them to ask for 'more'.

Nuts in May

Group size
Ten to 12 children.

What you need
A large space.

What to do
Divide the children into two lines, with at least one adult in each line. Arrange for the two lines to face each other, about 10 metres apart. One line starts by singing the first verse of the traditional song that has the same tune as 'Here We Go Round the Mulberry Bush' (Traditional).

Here we come gathering nuts in May, nuts in May, nuts in May.
Here we come gathering nuts in May, on a cold and frosty morning.

The other line then replies:

Who will you have for your nuts in May, nuts in May, nuts in May?
Who will you have for your nuts in May on a cold and frosty morning?

The first line then gathers together in a huddle and chooses a child's name from the other group.

We will have (child's name) for our nuts in May, nuts in May, nuts in May.
We will have (child's name) for our nuts in May on a cold and frosty morning.

Encourage the named child to join the first side. Stop to ask which line has the most people now and encourage the children to count each line.
Now the second line starts the song. They could ask for two children if they like. Now which line has the most people in it? Again, you can stop the rhyme, ask the children to estimate and count the heads together.

Special support
Start with just six of you altogether in two lines of three. After each verse, ask the child that you are targeting to guess which side has more children.

Extension
This traditional dance used to be sung with movement as well. Each side must move towards and away from the other side as they sing their verse.

LEARNING OBJECTIVES FOR ALL THE CHILDREN
● to say and use number names in order
● to find one more or one less than a number from 1 to 10.

INDIVIDUAL LEARNING TARGET
● to match the numeral '1' or '2' to the correct number of objects.

Countdown challenge

Group size
Ten to 20 children.

What you need
A hoop; ten coloured beanbags (or selection of other objects which are easy to count); set of number cards from 1 to 10; football rattle or party whistle.

What to do
Gather the children on the floor in a circle. Tell them that you are going to play a counting game. Place the hoop on the floor in the middle of the circle. Arrange three number cards, 1 to 3, on the floor, numeral side up.

Start with one of the older children. Place three beanbags in the circle and invite them to find the correct number card and place it in the circle with the beanbags. Cheer their success and wave your rattle.

Ensure that each child has a turn, then gradually increase the numbers in the sets and the range of number cards that you are matching. Choose tasks at the right level of ability for each child.

Play the game again, this time giving each child a number card and inviting them to place the correct number of beanbags into the hoop. Again, cheer their success.

Special support
Start with the number cards '1' and '2' only, and offer only one or two beanbags to match them to.

Extension
Invite older children to help you make the number cards. You can extend the set to 20 if you want to! Then challenge them to take one beanbag away from a hoop, or add one more beanbag to a hoop, and then to match this new set to the correct number card.

LINKS WITH HOME
Ask the parents or carers of any child that you are targeting to count 'One, two' as they help their child to put on their shoes and socks.

LEARNING OBJECTIVE FOR ALL THE CHILDREN
● to talk about, recognize and re-create simple patterns.

INDIVIDUAL LEARNING TARGET
● to continue a repetitive pattern sequence.

LINKS WITH HOME
Provide each child with a photocopiable sheet to take home for colouring games.

Sticker snakes

Group size
Two to four children.

What you need
A copy for each child of the photocopiable sheet on page 89; selection of stickers small enough for one to fit easily into each segment of the snakes (you need several of each kind of sticker); tray.

What to do
Spread the stickers out on a tray, colour side up and place them on a table. Encourage the children to sit down. Show each child one copy of the snakes and explain that they are twins, so they should look exactly the same. Encourage the children to watch as you select stickers, one for each section of the first snake.

Now ask the children to help you as you try to find matching stickers for the second snake, arranging them in the same order. The children can pass you the next one, or correct you if you are about to make a mistake. Then give each child a copy of the photocopiable sheet and ask them to make up their own pattern on a snake and to copy it exactly onto the 'twin'. Talk about the colours and the shapes as the children select and choose their stickers.

Special support
This is an excellent activity for breaking down into small steps. Work alongside the child that you are targeting. Choose one sticker for the first segment. Then encourage the child to find another that is the same for the second snake. Continue in this way, one segment at a time.

Make up one snake with a simple repetitive pattern, for example, one red circle and one yellow alternating. Provide the child with a limited choice of just red and yellow circles and help them as they try to make the second snake identical. You can do this with different shapes too.

Extension
Cut the snakes up and arrange them so that they are no longer parallel and aligned. Photocopy this new arrangement. Can the children still make their snakes identical?

LEARNING OBJECTIVE FOR ALL THE CHILDREN
● to use everyday words to describe position.

INDIVIDUAL LEARNING TARGET
● to respond appropriately to 'under' and 'over'.

Over our heads

Group size
12 to 24 children.

What you need
A parachute (or cut an old double sheet into a disc); large indoor space; one adult helper to every four children.

What to do
Take off your shoes so that you are in your socks, slippers or plimsolls. Show the children the parachute and encourage them to work out together how to hold onto an edge and make a big disc. When you have spaced yourself out around the parachute, sit down in a circle. Show the children how you can gently raise the parachute high and bring it down low. Sing this chant to a rising and a falling voice.

> We can go HIGH (pause for effect)
> We can go LOW (pause and repeat).

Invite individual children to do different things. Ask the first child to crawl over the parachute until they join the circle at the other side. Ask the next child to crawl under it. You can also ask groups of named children to stay under or on top of the parachute as the rest of you make gentle waves for them. Finish by raising the parachute high and then everyone slipping underneath it as it falls gently onto you.

Special support
Make sure that an adult is sitting next to the child that you are targeting and emphasize the key words 'under' and 'over' when you give them their instructions. If this is still difficult for the child, choose partners to do the task together so that there is another child for them to watch.

Extension
Invite older children to choose the next child and say what they should do for their task.

LINKS WITH HOME
Keep a running list of position words that the child you are targeting is learning. Ask parents and carers to practise these words at home and let you know how their child is getting on.

LEARNING OBJECTIVE FOR ALL THE CHILDREN
● in practical activities and discussion, to begin to use the vocabulary involved in adding and subtracting.

INDIVIDUAL LEARNING TARGET
● to use and respond to 'more'.

More, please!

Group size
One to four children at a time.

What you need
Your usual home corner with kitchen equipment, cups, saucers, play food, dolls, beds, table, chairs and so on.

What to do
Start by playing with the child that you are targeting and one other child in the home corner. Suggest that the first child make tea for you all. Help them to put out plates, one for each person in the house. Ask, 'Do we need more?'. Point to show who will have each plate so that you can help the child work out how many are needed. Do the same thing with the chairs around the table and with the saucers. Then help them to work out how many cups are needed for the saucers. Again, emphasize the key word 'more'. Share the food onto the plates, and encourage the child that you are targeting to ask whether the children want more. Keep the flow of the game as informal as possible, looking for natural opportunities to encourage the child to both respond to and to use the word 'more'. As more children join the game, look for more chairs, plates, cups and so on.

Special support
Once you feel that the child understands and is able to use the word 'more', look for other opportunities throughout the session to emphasize the word and encourage the child to use it. This is called 'generalization'.

Extension
Play a game with several dolls or teddies. Help the children to work out whether they need more or less plates and cups for them all.

LINKS WITH HOME
Ask parents and carers to encourage their children to ask for 'more, please' when playing together.

Brainy beakers

Group size
One child at a time.

What you need
A set of colourful stacking beakers.

What to do
This activity shows how you can use 'task analysis' (see heading 'Level' on page 21) to break down a simple task into easier steps. Start by introducing the stacking beakers to the child, all nesting together. How does the child play with these? Have a look at the typical ways in which developing children respond to this toy and decide at what level the child is playing at the moment. Play alongside them to encourage the next step in their thinking and learning. You can use this approach for all kinds of play activities and will find the booklet *Playladders* (page 96) useful to help you do this. For example:

- The child (Callum) looks at the beakers briefly.
- Callum looks at the beakers for three to four minutes as I play with them.

- Callum tries to pick the beakers up and shake them.
- Callum copies me as I tip them out.
- Callum will put a small beaker inside a larger one.
- Callum will put three or more beakers inside each other.
- Callum will copy me when I put a smaller beaker on top of a larger one.
- Callum will add the top beaker to the tower I have made.
- Callum will stack three beakers when given a choice of the three.
- Callum will stack all the beakers by size.
- Callum will give me a 'big' or a 'little' beaker from a choice of two very different ones.

LEARNING OBJECTIVE FOR ALL THE CHILDREN
- to use language such as 'bigger' and 'smaller' to compare two sizes.

INDIVIDUAL LEARNING TARGET
- to grade stacking beakers by size.

LINKS WITH HOME
Encourage the parents or carers of the child that you are targeting to join a local toy library and borrow toys for grading and stacking.

Special support
Coloured stacking beakers are amazingly adaptable for teaching all kinds of early learning skills. Use them to teach colour matching, building, counting, scooping, pouring, imagining and remembering (by hiding a small toy under one beaker), sharing and turn-taking (by taking turns to add the next beaker to the stack).

Extension
Play at size-grading pebbles, toy animals, and even a row of children!

One more step

Group size
Two or three children.

What you need
A series of paving stones or floor tiles which are one child's stride between each other (you can also use carpet squares which do not slip on a carpet surface); chalks, paints or inks for marking.

What to do
This game involves counting steps, careful listening and number recognition. Number five consecutive squares 1 to 5. Gather the children in a row, all holding hands with you. Tell them that you are going to play a counting game. Can they see the numbers? Face the first tile and chant 'one, two, three, four, five' as you take five strides together from tile to tile. Now help them balance as you have fun taking five strides backwards, counting 'five, four, three, two, one'. Challenge a child to count to two, taking two strides. Are they standing on number 2? Check to see. Now can they take one more step? See where they have landed. Give each child a task to do, taking steps forwards and backwards, then looking at and saying their new number. After a while, you can ask the other children to guess which number is 'one less' or 'one more'.

Special support
The point of this activity is that early one-to-one correspondence when counting (counting one number for one object) comes most easily when there is an action involved. Counting steps is an ideal way to encourage the child to chant 'one, two, three' while taking one, two, three steps. You can make sure that the child whom you are targeting has a task that they can succeed at by keeping the number low, holding a hand, and praising success.

Extension
Make number snakes on the floor that have 20 segments. Roll a dice and take that number of strides. How many throws does it take to reach the end of the snake?

KNOWLEDGE AND UNDERSTANDING OF THE WORLD

These activities help children with learning difficulties to develop confidence in exploring and finding out. This chapter looks at introducing new vocabulary and extending the children's concentration.

Rainy days

Group size
Three or four children.

What you need
Raincoats; hats; wellington boots; umbrellas; towels; drying space.

What to do
Warn the children to come prepared on the next rainy day so that you can enjoy a walk in the rain together. Spend some time getting ready as you help the children to put on their coats and hats and find the right feet for their boots. Talk about why you need to dress up in the rain. Why aren't you putting on your sun-glasses? What would happen if you wore a sun-hat? Why do we need umbrellas?

Now move outside together and enjoy a walk around the playground, the garden or the block. Make sure that you have enough supervision for safety and hold hands as you cross any roads.

Spend a moment standing still and closing your eyes. What can you hear? Listen to the wheels of the passing cars, the water in the drains, the rain on the roofs. Hold up your faces and feel the raindrops. Step through the puddles and watch your wet boot prints. Encourage the children to notice, look, listen and feel.

Come back inside and continue talking together as you dry your faces and hang up your clothes to dry.

Special support
This activity provides opportunities for talking very simply about the weather. It also allows you to spend time focusing on dressing and undressing skills, staying close to the child and providing just the right amount of assistance that they need to do it independently. Encourage all the child's efforts.

Extension
Support the children as they design their own daily weather chart.

LEARNING OBJECTIVES FOR ALL THE CHILDREN
● to look closely at similarities, differences and change
● to observe, find out about and identify features in the natural world.

INDIVIDUAL LEARNING TARGETS
● to think about the changing weather and identify 'rain' and 'sun'
● to put on coat, boots and hat independently.

LINKS WITH HOME
Suggest adding two little dots over the big toes of the children's wellington boots to help them choose the right foot. Correction fluid works well and does not wash off in the rain.

LEARNING OBJECTIVE FOR ALL THE CHILDREN
● to begin to know about their own cultures and those of others.

INDIVIDUAL LEARNING TARGETS
● to handle and explore the rice tray
● to experience new tastes.

Rice is nice

Group size
All the children at different times.

What you need
A small sand tray or washing-up bowl part-filled with rice; small pourers and containers; pens; assortment of Chinese tastes to sample such as rice crackers, crispy noodles, spring rolls and fortune cookies; chopsticks; small Chinese-style bowls; jasmine tea; percussion instruments such as drums, triangles and wooden blocks; traditional Chinese music on a tape or CD; cassette or CD player.

What to do
Celebrate Chinese New Year at your setting. Instead of a sand tray, put out a rice tray and enjoy the feeling as you pour the grains over each other's hands. Make rice shakers by sealing rice into yoghurt pots and decorating them with Chinese symbols.

At snack time, enjoy some new tastes from Chinese bowls. Can you use the chopsticks? Do you like the tastes? Encourage the children to try small amounts and to share the food around.

At music time, play some traditional percussion sounds to your Chinese music. March around the room with your instruments. If you do not have any Chinese music, play a rhythmic tune on the black notes on a piano or keyboard to simulate a Chinese dance.

Special support
Enjoy the touches and the tastes together and use simple commentary to help the child link actions and feelings to words.

Extension
Make stick puppets of a rat, an ox, a tiger, a hare, a dragon, a snake, a horse, a sheep, a monkey, a cockerel, a dog and a pig for a special 'Yuan Tan' dance for the Chinese New Year.

LINKS WITH HOME
Invite families and members of the local Chinese community to visit the children and talk to them about the New Year. Make copies of the photocopiable sheet on page 90 for the children to take home and share with their families. Check with parents and carers to see if any of the children have allergies or dietary requirements before tasting food.

KNOWLEDGE & UNDERSTANDING OF THE WORLD

LEARNING OBJECTIVES FOR ALL THE CHILDREN
- to find out about their environment
- to enjoy selecting tools and techniques when hairdressing.

INDIVIDUAL LEARNING TARGET
- to play passively with other children.

LINKS WITH HOME
Sometimes parents and carers find it very difficult to take their children for a haircut because the children are frightened or throw a tantrum there. Explain to parents and carers that playing 'hairdressers' will help the experience to become more familiar and relaxing for a child with particular difficulties.

Hairdressing salon

Group size
Three or four children.

What you need
Props for a hairdressing corner; very soft brushes and large combs; towels; foam rollers; safe mirrors; washing-up bowls; selection of hair decorations such as scrunchies, bands and clips.

What to do
Move into the hairdressing corner to start the game rolling. Be prepared to sit back for a while as you are groomed and decorated! Encourage all the children to visit the hair salon or to take a turn at being a hairdresser. Admire yourselves in the mirrors. Talk about the children's own experiences of seeing hairdressers, and develop the game with further props and ideas.

Help the children to think of the sequences involved: first the hair is combed, then washed, then dried, then styled. Lead up to a grand fashion parade at the end of the session.

Special support
This activity was chosen because it can be a gentle way of including a child with profound and multiple learning difficulties. Stay with them at all times and encourage the other children to gently brush or stroke their hair. Point out the ways in which the child that you are targeting is showing how happy they are: 'Look how still Jos is lying – he really enjoys it', 'Can you see how Danielle is giggling – she likes your gentle brushing' and so on. Be aware of any discomfort so that you can stop the activity when the child that you are targeting has had enough.

Extension
Paint pictures of amazing hair-styles or model them in play dough.

KNOWLEDGE & UNDERSTANDING OF THE WORLD

LEARNING OBJECTIVE FOR ALL THE CHILDREN
● to observe, find out about, and identify features in the place where they live.

INDIVIDUAL LEARNING TARGETS
● to understand that 'money' needs to be exchanged when shopping
● to identify a 1p and a 2p coin.

Buying and selling

Group size
Two children.

What you need
A selection of coins (1p, 2p, 5p, 10p, 20p, 50p, £1); shopping corner with price labels.

What to do
Tell parents and carers that you will be thinking and finding out about shopping this week. Explain that you would like to take the children to the local shop, two at a time.

Introduce the activity by talking about the shops in your local area. Ask questions such as, 'Where does Mum buy the bread?', 'Where do you go to buy clothes?', 'Where do people go to buy food for their families?', 'What do you need to buy food with?' and so on. Talk about money and introduce a selection of coins. Ask, 'Which is the £1 coin?', 'Which is the 1p coin?', 'Which coin would buy the most sweets?' and so on.

Set up a shop role-play area for the children to play a buying and selling game. Mark the items with 1p or 2p and give the children real 1p and 2p coins to play with.

Follow this with a session where all the children plan a coming school fête or fund-raising event. What could you buy and sell there? Visit the local shops, two children at a time with one or two adults to hold their hands. Help the children to buy 'penny sweets' for the sweet stall, counting them into the bag and counting out the corresponding number of 1p coins.

Special support
Teach the child that you are targeting to identify 1p and 2p coins. When buying sweets, just start with counting out three sweets and exchanging these for three 1p coins.

Extension
Older children will be able to handle and count with 2p coins as well.

LINKS WITH HOME
Ask parents and carers to encourage their children to handle small amounts of money when they are shopping for low-cost items.

Time of day

Group size
Three or four children.

What you need
A copy of the photocopiable sheet on page 91 for each child; model or card clock-face with movable hands; pencils.

What to do
Gather the children together and talk about times of the day. What time do they get up in the morning? What time do they go to bed? You will probably have to do the thinking here, showing the children the clock hands to represent when the children usually get up and when they go to bed.

Now talk about what happens in between. As the children talk, help them to sequence their ideas so that you begin to build up a series of activities through the day.

Think about a session at your setting. Again, help the children to talk about the typical routine until you have a simple timetable in your minds. Assist them with drawing the clock hands onto their clocks on their photocopiable sheets to represent the different times during the session, or make up your own timetable if it is different.

Special support
Children with special needs often have great difficulty in associating time with events and in sequencing events in their minds. Provide a simple visual timetable, with pictures from left to right, to give them a concrete idea of what happens next and what activity follows another. Begin to teach certain familiar clock times for definite times of day. You can introduce digital clock times if this is more appropriate for your situation.

Extension
Older children can begin to tell the time to the nearest o'clock.

LEARNING OBJECTIVE FOR ALL THE CHILDREN
● to find out about past and present events in their own lives.

INDIVIDUAL LEARNING TARGET
● to associate clock times with the start and end of the session.

LINKS WITH HOME
Send the completed photocopiable sheet home and suggest that parents and carers ask their children to recount their session.

LEARNING OBJECTIVE FOR ALL THE CHILDREN
● to build and construct, selecting appropriate resources, and adapting work when necessary.

INDIVIDUAL LEARNING TARGETS
● to construct a simple beam bridge out of bricks
● to copy a simple construction.

LINKS WITH HOME
Ask parents and parents to point out bridges to their childrenin your local area. Who or what goes under them? Who or what goes over them?

Building bridges

Group size
Two or three children.

What you need
A selection of building bricks in various shapes; selection of small cars and trains.

What to do
Place the bricks in a clear floor area and show them to the children. Tell them that you have a special job for them to do today. Explain that you would like them to make you as many bridges as they can and that your car (or train) will test them out. Make sure that they understand what a bridge is, and show them how your car can go under the bridge and also over it. Leave them while they work out how they can make as many bridges as possible using the bricks. Return to encourage them and also to try the bridges out, passing your car over and under.

Now supply a selection of cars and trains for the children to develop their game.

Special support
Show the child that you are targeting how to make a simple bridge of three bricks, with one each side and one on top. At first, they are likely to place the two supports next to each other. Use your car to show that a space is needed beneath the bridge. Encourage the child as they work out how to build a structure that is successful as a bridge. Emphasize the key words 'under' and 'over' as you play with the cars together.

Extension
Provide a selection of materials and challenge the children to make as large a bridge as possible.

Tiling time

Group size
Three or four children.

What you need
Clay; potter's tools for rolling, poking, marking, chiselling, cutting, or adapt your own from your modelling tools (this activity can also be done with play dough, though the tiles will not be as permanent).

What to do
Introduce the children to the clay and enjoy its feel as you manipulate it into shapes. Mould the clay for a while to make it soft, wetting your hands to make the clay more moist as you need to. Ask each child to select a tool for making the clay flat. Help them to choose the roller and show them how to press and roll until they have a flat sheet. Mark the shape of a tile onto the sheet and then encourage the child to select tools to impress, chisel and mark a pattern into their tile.

   If you have facilities to bake or dry, to paint and to varnish the tiles, then these make a lovely permanent record to add to a wall or a window sill.

Special support
The child that you are targeting may still be at a stage of loving to feel and to touch. Enjoy the process of this activity for all its exploration as well as the final product.

Extension
Older children might like to design a tile first and then select the most appropriate tools for making up the design.

Wonderful windmills

Group size
Two or three children.

What you need
A copy of the photocopiable sheet on page 92; hand-held pin windmill from a novelty shop or fairground; felt-tipped pens or crayons; scissors; glue; a 15cm length of dowelling rod for each child; drawing pins.

What to do
Show the children your windmill. See if they can work out themselves how to make it turn. They might run along and hold it high. They might swing it through the air. They might blow it.

Now suggest that the children make their own windmill to take home. Give each child a copy of the photocopiable sheet and encourage them to make the square shape as colourful as they can. Help them to cut out the shape and cut along the thick lines.

Assist the children with folding the four corners into the centre of the windmill (see right). Glue these down and allow the glue to dry (this will stiffen the centre and make the windmill spin more easily). Place a drawing pin through the centre, working the hole slightly larger than the pin to help it spin. Push this firmly into one end of the dowel. Warn the children to be careful and not to remove the pin.

LEARNING OBJECTIVES FOR ALL THE CHILDREN
● to ask questions about why things happen and how things work
● to construct a simple windmill.

INDIVIDUAL LEARNING TARGET
● to blow a windmill in order to make it turn.

LINKS WITH HOME
Suggest other activities for practising blowing skills at home, for example, using a straw and a ping-pong ball to play 'Blow football'.

Special support
Use four-holed scissors to teach cutting skills. Place your hands behind the child's so that you can prompt the open and shut movements.

Extension
Talk about windmills and make a large model out of boxes and tubes.

Harry Hedgehog

Group size
Three or four children.

What you need
A copy of the photocopiable sheet on page 93 for each child; cotton-wool roll; plastic cups; sheets of card; coloured pens; glue; mustard and cress seed; scissors for the children and for yourself; Cellophane; picture of a hedgehog.

What to do
Before you start this activity, cut the plastic cups down so that they are only about 2cm deep. Cut discs of cotton wool the same size as the cups. Photocopy or trace templates of Harry Hedgehog onto sheets of card from the template on the photocopiable sheet on page 93.

Link this activity to work that you are doing on 'growing things'. Gather the children around and show them your hedgehog picture. Would they like to make a 'Harry Hedgehog' of their own? It would be funny to make one out of seeds and watch how they grow!

Help each child to cut out the outline of Harry Hedgehog, colour it and write their name underneath. Ask them to place a disc of cotton wool in their shallow cup and to glue this onto the body. Place all the 'hedgehogs' on one side to dry.

Later, help the children to moisten the cotton wool with some drops of water and to scatter some seed on the top. Place these in a dim but warm corner and, once the children have gone home, cover the tops with Cellophane.

Enjoy inspecting your 'hedgehogs' every day as you watch the seeds growing. Remove the Cellophane once they have germinated and encourage the children to keep them moist.

Special support
Fine motor control might be difficult. Encourage gentle watering by using a plastic container with the lid pierced with small holes. Help the child that you are targeting to aim the water carefully at Harry's back.

Extension
Find ways of recording the daily progress of your seeds.

LEARNING OBJECTIVE FOR ALL THE CHILDREN
● to observe, find out about, and identify features of the natural world.

INDIVIDUAL LEARNING TARGET
● to observe and talk about growing seeds.

LINKS WITH HOME
Take Harry home to make a nutritious snack or sandwich. He can always be used to grow another batch!

KNOWLEDGE & UNDERSTANDING OF THE WORLD

**LEARNING
OBJECTIVES FOR
ALL THE CHILDREN**
● to look closely at
similarities and
change
● to observe and
identify features in
the place where they
go to nursery.

**INDIVIDUAL
LEARNING TARGET**
● to label six things
which they can see
outside of the
window.

LINKS WITH HOME
Send copies of the
photocopiable sheet
home for the children
to share with their
parents or carers. Ask
the parents or carers
of the child that you
are targeting to
provide a simple
commentary about
everything the child
could see from a car
or bus window when
out on a journey.

Through the window

Group size
Eight to 12 children.

What you need
An enlarged copy of the photocopiable sheet on page 94; clear view
from a window.

What to do
Gather the children together and read the poem on the photocopiable
sheet. Discuss the view in the poem and start to compare it with the
view from a window in your own setting. Gather around the window
and invite the children to list everything that they can see. Encourage
more and more ideas as the children notice new things and make
connections with other views that they have seen. Prompt them with
questions such as, 'Do you have a bedroom window at home?', 'What
can you see from it?' and so on. Encourage them to close their eyes and
try to remember.

Special support
Children with learning difficulties sometimes find it hard to remember
and to visualize. Encourage them to list familiar objects that they can
see. Ask them 'yes' and 'no' questions about their bedroom windows,
such as, 'Can you see the street?', 'Can you see cars?' and so on.

Extension
Encourage the children to draw the views they have from their windows.

PHYSICAL DEVELOPMENT

Children with learning difficulties sometimes have problems in moving, balancing and co-ordinating. In this chapter you will find a range of practical ideas for supporting them in their physical activities at your setting.

Stringing along

Group size
All the children at different times.

What you need
A ball of soft string; Blu-Tack; 'treasure chest' to rummage in, with items such as shiny and glittery fabrics, 'jewels', feathered hats and so on.

What to do
Before the children arrive, make a string track which weaves around corners from play area to play area. Place the treasure chest and its contents at the end of the track. Secure the string in place with Blu-Tack every few paces.

As the children arrive, challenge them to follow the trail, toe to toe. Can they balance carefully all the way without moving the string? Encourage them to rummage in the treasure chest when they reach the end of the trail and to dress up in some of the hats and fabrics.

During the next session, suggest that the child whom you are targeting help you to lay another trail. This time, lay the trail in a hall or open floor space, leading from safety mat to safety mat or bench to bench. Challenge the child to balance carefully along it for at least three steps, staying close to encourage them. Now invite everyone in to follow the 'obstacle course' that you have set up, balancing along the string from obstacle to obstacle around the room.

Special support
Walking toe to toe can be difficult to master for a child whose development is delayed. Start with a straight line and encourage them to hold their arms wide for balance. Support their hands lightly and gradually withdraw your support. Keep the distance short and achievable, celebrating their success.

Extension
Send a small group of children ahead to lay a trail for others to follow. Use chalk lines instead of string if you carry out this activity outside.

Traffic-lights

Group size
Three or four children.

What you need
A playground outside; collection of toy vehicles; road sign (the shape of a lollipop baton) with 'GO' on one side coloured green and 'STOP' on the other side coloured red; chalk.

What to do
Chalk a road in a figure of '8' right across the playground, which will have a crossroads in the centre. Invite a few children to ride around on the toy vehicles while you stand at the crossroads and direct the traffic. Show a car the red sign when you want it to stop and the green when you want it to pass. Keep the game fun and elaborate it as it develops. You might expand this game by dressing up as a police officer and using hand signals. Praise the drivers for driving safely and stopping when you tell them to.

Encourage the children to use a right- or left-hand signal as they wait to indicate which way they would like to turn at the crossroads.

Special support
At first, use words as well as the signs or signals for 'stop' and 'go'. In time, encourage the child that you are targeting to look at the sign or signal on its own. Try using a white card saying 'STOP' or 'GO'. Can they still understand it?

Extension
Talk about other road signs and their meanings. Use your sign as a novel way of making everyone stop what they are doing when you need to talk to them.

LEARNING OBJECTIVE FOR ALL THE CHILDREN
● to move with control and co-ordination

INDIVIDUAL LEARNING TARGET
● to imitate a simple action

Panda and Ted

Group size
Eight to 12 children.

What you need
A large panda; large teddy; open space

What to do
Gather the children in your large space and ask them to sit down on the floor while you introduce the game. Tell them to listen very carefully because everything that Panda tells them to do, they should do. But everything that Ted tells them to do, they should not do!

Ask the children to stand up. Hold up Panda in the air and make him jump up and down and say, 'Panda says jump up and down!'. Look to see if the children are copying Panda. Now make Panda turn around. 'Panda says turn around!'. Again the children should copy him. After three or four actions from Panda, lift up Ted and make it clear from your serious face and shaking your head that this is something that the children should *not* do. Say, 'Ted says lie down' or 'Ted says run around'. Introduce Panda again and, as the game progresses, give the children fewer clues. Can they still remember? When you have finished playing the game, congratulate the children and have a rest.

Special support
This is a more concrete version of the familiar game 'Simon says'. Stay close to the child and encourage them to look and to listen carefully. Keep the session short and end on a successful note.

Extension
Play 'Simon says'. In this game, the children join in if the command starts with 'Simon says' but ignore it if it is on its own, for example, 'Simon says run around', as opposed to 'Run around'.

LINKS WITH HOME
Encourage parents and carers to have a toy at home through which they can say, for example, 'Put your toys away' when their children are blissfully ignoring them!

LEARNING OBJECTIVE FOR ALL THE CHILDREN
● to show awareness of space, themselves and others.

INDIVIDUAL LEARNING TARGET
● to think independently of an action.

LINKS WITH HOME
Suggest that the parents or carers of the child that you are targeting help their child learn to imitate simple actions by playing a copying game in a mirror.

Stamping feet

Group size
Six to 20 children.

What you need
An open space.

What to do
Take the children to an open indoor space and sit in a wide circle on the floor. Introduce the game to the group by singing the song below, putting in your own name, to the tune of the traditional song 'Have You Seen the Muffin Man?'.

> Mrs Bright is stamping feet, stamping feet, stamping feet
> Mrs Bright is stamping feet, let's all do the same!

Ask everyone to stand up and copy as you sing together:

> Everyone is stamping feet, stamping feet, stamping feet
> Everyone is stamping feet, now sit down together!

Sit down wherever you are on the floor. Invite a child to choose an action and demonstrate it to the group while you sing another verse.

> Parveen is hopping now, hopping now, hopping now
> Parveen is hopping now, let's all do the same!

Stand up and join in, singing the second verse again. Continue until everyone has had a turn. Encourage the children to think of a new action each time. If you cannot describe it, just sing 'Jonathan is doing this' and so on.

Special support
Keep the group size small and invite the child that you are targeting to have a turn near the beginning. When they are copying, encourage them to watch what the other children are doing.

Extension
Encourage the children to move around the room in a line and to think of different ways of moving along. Have a new leader at the front of the line for each new action.

LEARNING OBJECTIVES FOR ALL THE CHILDREN
● to show awareness of space
● to aim with control and co-ordination

INDIVIDUAL LEARNING TARGET
● to knock down three skittles at a distance of one metre

Skittle alley

Group size
Two children.

What you need
A set of plastic skittles; large sponge ball; open space with a hard floor.

What to do
Ask the children to sit down on the floor facing one another with their legs wide apart in front of them. Start with the children fairly close to one another and show them how to roll the ball, funneling it between their legs to make it easier to catch and to return. Gradually move further apart as the children become better at aiming and catching. Then encourage them to kneel up and see whether they can still roll the ball to one another.

Finally, let the children play a partner game with one child setting up the skittles and the other child rolling the ball to knock them down. Encourage them to take it in turns to roll the ball and to place the skittles.

Special support
Break the task down into smaller skills, teaching each skill a step at a time, for example, when the children are rolling the ball to one another, sit behind the child that you are targeting so that you can help them catch and roll back the ball, hand over hand. Start with just one or two skittles and have them no more than a metre away from the child. Begin by rolling a large sponge ball and work up to managing to knock the skittles over with a smaller ball.

Extension
Challenge older children to announce how many skittles they have knocked over each turn and to add them up as they go along.

LINKS WITH HOME
Encourage parents and carers to sit with their children and practise rolling a ball to each other.

To and fro

Group size
Three or four children.

What you need
Cylindrical containers made from card, or large empty plastic soft-drinks bottles; stickers; colourful pieces of Fablon; rice; pasta shapes; dry pulses (not red kidney beans); funnels; strong glue (adult use).

What to do
Place all the materials except the glue on a table. Help the children to choose patches of Fablon and stickers to decorate the outside of the cylinders or bottles. Encourage each child to stick these onto the outside of their cylinder. Make sure that the decorations are stuck down well so that the surface remains smooth (so that it will roll). Encourage the children to part-fill a container with pulses, rice and pasta so that an interesting sound is made when it is shaken. Show them how to use the funnels with their bottles. Place their rollers on one side and secure the lids with strong glue so that the materials are sealed into their containers.

Take the rollers onto a smooth surface and try rolling them along. Play the partner rolling game in 'Skittle alley' on page 69 and enjoy the sound that the rollers make as they pass from partner to partner.

Finally, use the containers as rainmakers during music time, tipping them carefully from side to side and listening to the 'falling rain'.

Special support
Make the surface of the roller bright and reflective as this activity is especially motivating for children who may have a sensory difficulty as well as a learning difficulty. Let them enjoy the sounds as the roller rolls and swishes.

Extension
Think together about how you can make your rollers into more effective rainmakers. Introduce obstacles to the flow that cause the pulses to catch and tumble.

LEARNING OBJECTIVES FOR ALL THE CHILDREN
● to handle tools and construction materials with increasing control
● to show awareness of space, of themselves and of others.

INDIVIDUAL LEARNING TARGET
● to roll a cylinder to and fro with one other child.

LINKS WITH HOME
Ask the parents or carers of the child that you are targeting to use the rollers at home to play a rolling game.

LEARNING OBJECTIVE FOR ALL THE CHILDREN
● to recognize the importance of keeping healthy and those things which contribute to this.

INDIVIDUAL LEARNING TARGET
● to taste and enjoy several fruit.

Fruit salad

Group size
Three or four children.

What you need
Chopping boards; blunt knives; paper plates; selection of seasonal fresh fruit from around the world; sharp fruit knife (adult use); serving bowl; small bowls; spoons; carton of pure orange, apple or pineapple juice; plastic film covering.

What to do
Before carrying out this activity, check for any food allergies or dietary requirements. Arrange the selection of fruit and knives on a table. Take the children to wash their hands. As they wash and dry their hands, talk about why it is necessary to wash hands before touching food. Remind the children not to lick their fingers now that their hands are clean.

Gather around the table and talk about the fruit that you have. Ask the children questions such as, 'Who has tasted this?', 'Which do you like?' and so on. Involve them in washing and preparing the fruit as much as possible, perhaps asking them to wash the apples or try to peel a satsuma. Suggest that you make a pattern with pieces of fruit on a paper plate for the children to take home. As you work, talk about why fruit is such a healthy food. What other healthy foods can the children think of?

Use the sharp knife to peel and prepare the fruit, then pass smaller pieces to the children for any final cutting and shaping with their blunt knives. Show them how the pieces of fruit might be arranged in a face or a pattern. Put the plates on one side and cover with film, ready to take home.

Cut up the rest of the fruit and mix it in a bowl with some pure fruit juice. Place this in the fridge until snack time. Sample different tastes by serving each child a bowl of fruit salad. Encourage them to try tiny tastes if they are not sure.

Special support
Some children remain faddy about food and tastes for a long time. Making the food into novelty shapes and patterns is one way of encouraging them to feel more adventurous when eating.

Extension
Help the children to make nutritious salad sandwiches out of wholemeal bread. Talk about the differences between white foods and wholemeal foods and which ones are healthier.

LINKS WITH HOME
If any of the children are reluctant eaters, suggest to their parents or carers that they serve fruit in different ways, for example, as a face to encourage their children to it.

PHYSICAL DEVELOPMENT · PHYSICAL DEVELOPMENT · PHYSICAL DEVELOPMENT

LEARNING OBJECTIVE FOR ALL THE CHILDREN
● to move with confidence, control and co-ordination.

INDIVIDUAL LEARNING TARGET
● to copy a large body movement.

Dinosaur hunt

Group size
All the children, with a ratio of one adult to six children.

What you need
A wide open space; large plastic dinosaur.

What to do
This activity is a simplified version of the story *We're Going on a Bear Hunt* by Michael Rosen (Walker Books). Hide a plastic dinosaur somewhere in the room so that you can 'find' it at the end of the dinosaur hunt. Make sure that all the children have a chance to join in, regardless of mobility.

Tell the children what you are going to do and that they must repeat everything you say. Make sure that you have plenty of adults to help the children to copy you.

'We're going on a dinosaur hunt.' (Children repeat as you all march around.)
'Isn't it fun!' (Children repeat as you all rub your hands together with enthusiasm.)
'Lovely weather!' (Children repeat as you all point up to the clear sky.)
'Oh oh...' (Children repeat as you all stop still.)
'Grass.' (Children repeat.)
'Tall, wavy grass.' (Children repeat as you all make a swishing hand movement.)
'Got to go through it.' (Children repeat as you all make huge steps, saying 'Swish swish swish'.)

Repeat the rhyme replacing 'Grass' and 'Tall, wavy grass' with the following:

Verse 2: 'Mud' and 'Dark squelchy mud' (make squelchy wellington-boot steps)
Verse 3: 'Nettles' and 'Tall stingy nettles' (jump over them saying 'Ow! Ow! Ow!')
Verse 4: 'A cave' and 'A dark echoey cave' (feel your way in making echo noises)
Verse 5: 'A dinosaur!' and 'Let's run home!'.
Reverse all the sounds as you run back to base, starting with echoey noises, then nettles, then mud, then tall wavy grass, finally arriving safely home and celebrating.

Special support
Ask an adult helper to stay close to the child that you are targeting in order to help them imitate and move and to encourage them constantly.

Extension
Ask the children to think of some more verses.

LINKS WITH HOME
Suggest that parents and carers try this rhyme to make an otherwise dull walk more interesting.

LEARNING OBJECTIVE FOR ALL THE CHILDREN
● to move with control, co-ordination and rhythm.

INDIVIDUAL LEARNING TARGET
● to join in a simple one–two beat with hands and feet.

Cobbler, cobbler

Group size
Eight to 20 children.

What you need
Large work boots or heavy shoes; extra adults to help with shoes.

What to do
Encourage the children to kneel down in a circle with their two hands on the floor. Put your own two hands into your heavy boots, and raise them up and down to tramp a strong one–two rhythm. Can the children make the same rhythm? Try it with your hands and then encourage the children to take their shoes off and put them on their hands. Chant this rhyme as you 'walk' your hands:

Cobbler, cobbler, mend my shoe,
Get it done by half-past two.
(Traditional)

Repeat once or twice more and then move on to other one–two rhythm chants that you all know, for example:

Down at the bottom of the deep blue sea,
Catching fishes for my tea,
How many fishes can you see?
One... two... three... .
(Traditional)

Now stand up and stomp your boots as the children follow you around a circle, chanting and stomping to the beat.

Special support
Younger or less able children might enjoy having arms or legs swung to the beat, or bouncing when held in a standing position.

Extension
Select a tape or CD with a strong one–two rhythm such as 'The Grand Old Duke of York' and ask the children to choose a percussion instrument. Use a loud drum to keep the beat. If any of the children have already developed a sense of regular rhythm, encourage them to drum to the beat for you.

LINKS WITH HOME
When parents and carers are out on a walk with their children, encourage them to hold hands and chant and march together to make it more interesting.

LEARNING OBJECTIVE FOR ALL THE CHILDREN
● to move with confidence, safety, control and co-ordination.

INDIVIDUAL LEARNING TARGET
● to kick a ball.

Goal!

Group size
Three children at a time.

What you need
A large indoor space; two goalposts to shoot between, such as two tables or chairs draped with blankets; large sponge ball; whistle; a football rattle; pumps or trainers for the children.

What to do
Set up the goalposts two-thirds of the way down the open space or hall. Help the children to change into suitable footwear for the football game and practise kicking the ball between the goalposts. Then set up a 'penalty shoot-out'. Ask one child to go to the far end of the room, well behind the goalposts to return the ball, one 'supporter' to stand on the 'sideline' with the rattle, and one to stand in front of the goalposts ready to kick. Let that child have as many turns as is necessary at kicking the ball successfully into the goal. Encourage the supporter to cheer and rattle from the sideline when a goal is scored. Change places until everyone has enjoyed several turns. Use your whistle to signal 'Goal'! and 'Change places!' each time a goal is scored.

Special support
Use 'task analysis' (see heading 'Level' on page 21) to make the task easier for a child with learning difficulties. At first, they may be able to kick a stationary ball between the posts if they are standing right in front of the goal. In time, they will be able to aim and kick from further away. In yet more time, they will be able to run and kick in one flowing movement. See which stage the child that you are targeting has reached, and encourage the next steps.

Extension
Introduce a 'goal keeper' for older and more able children.

LINKS WITH HOME
Encourage the parents or carers of the child that you are targeting to help their child practise ball skills at home, too.

CREATIVE DEVELOPMENT

This chapter provides activities for encouraging creative development in young children. Art and craft can offer opportunities for enjoying sensory play and there are ideas for involving children with learning difficulties fully and usefully.

LEARNING OBJECTIVE FOR ALL THE CHILDREN
● to recognize and explore how sounds can be changed.

INDIVIDUAL LEARNING TARGET
● to turn towards a sound.

Soundabout

Group size
16 to 24 children.

What you need
A soft rope, long enough to go all around the circle and tied with a knot; four adult helpers; tambourine; jingle bells; shaker; clappers (or similar).

What to do
Gather the children in a circle, sitting on the floor. Invite four helpers to sit at four points of the compass outside the circle, each with one of the four instruments hidden behind their back. Place the rope in the children's hands so that each child is holding it with a slight slack in it. Practise passing the rope around, showing the children which direction it should go. As they pass the rope, the knot will transfer from child to child. Teach the children the rhyme below to the tune of 'Here We Go Looby Loo' (Traditional) from *Okki-tokki-unga* chosen by Beatrice Harrop (A & C Black) as you pass the rope around.

Passing the rope around,
Passing the rope around,
When the music stops,
Who will find the sound?

At the end of each verse, observe which child is holding the know or is closest to it. Wink at one of the four helpers to indicate who should play their instrument. Invite the child with the knot to point towards the sound as the helper that you have designated shakes their instrument softly behind their back.

Special support
Start by asking the adult helpers to play the instruments rather loudly when it is the turn of the child that you are targeting. In time, they can make softer sounds as the child becomes better at locating sounds.

Extension
Invite older children to identify which musical instrument is being played by the helper.

LINKS WITH HOME
Encourage the parents or carers of the child that you are targeting to play a 'Hide the sound' game at home, for example, blowing a whistle behind a curtain and noting whether the child can locate it.

LEARNING OBJECTIVES FOR ALL THE CHILDREN
● to recognize and explore how sounds can be changed
● to match movements to music.

INDIVIDUAL LEARNING TARGET
● to carry out a repeated action to music.

Tiddly tum tum tum

Group size
Eight to 12 children.

What you need
A selection of tambourines, shakers and bells.

What to do
Encourage the children to choose an instrument each and to sit on the floor in a circle. Ask older or more able children to 'tell your hands to put your instrument on the floor and sit still on your laps'. Ask the child that you are targeting to play their instrument, showing them if necessary, for example, shaking their bell.

Encourage all the children to copy the action with their own instrument as you sing together, to the tune of 'Auld Lang Syne':

> We're shaking now, we're shaking now,
> We're shaking, shaking now
> We're shaking now, we're shaking now,
> We're shaking, shaking now.

Repeat the verse a second time to the words 'Tiddly tum tum tum' and so on.

Encourage a new child to choose an action for each verse and all the other children to mirror it, for example, tapping their knee with their instrument, or beating it with their hand, or tapping it on their elbow. Then encourage each child to try to think of new ways of making sounds with their instrument.

If you cannot think of how to put a child's action into words, then sing 'We're doing this' and so on.

Special support
This activity will also encourage positive self-esteem in the child that you are targeting as they will see all the children taking up and copying their action. Be especially aware of developing positive self-esteem and confidence in any child who is experiencing learning difficulties.

Extension
Let the children play a sound-mirroring game in pairs. Encourage them to take it in turns to choose an action to each verse. Their partners should copy them as everyone sings the song.

LINKS WITH HOME
Encourage the parents or carers of the child that you are targeting to sing nursery rhymes with repeated sounds, such as 'Old MacDonald Had a Farm'. These are sometimes the first words that a child with developmental difficulties can join in with.

LEARNING OBJECTIVES FOR ALL THE CHILDREN
● to explore texture in two and three dimensions
● to respond in a variety of ways to what they feel.

INDIVIDUAL LEARNING TARGET
● to make a simple careful handprint.

Sandy handies

Group size
Two children.

What you need
Aprons; shallow tray of washable glue; part-filled tray of fine dry sand; sheets of coloured sugar paper; bowls of warm soapy water; towels; pencils; pouring beaker; glitter.

What to do
Place the two trays on the table. Add glitter to the sand tray. Place the bowls of soapy water and towels adjacent to your work area.
Encourage each child to put their apron on and to choose a coloured sheet of sugar paper. Help them to write or trace their name on it. Place the paper on the table. Show the children how to place a hand in the glue and to press a single firm handprint onto a sheet of paper. Then help each child to do the same. Now encourage them to wash and dry their hands.
   Hold each child's handprint picture over the tray of sand and encourage them to use the pouring beaker to gently pour sand over it to make a sandy handprint. Leave the prints to dry.
   When the handprints are dry, enjoy looking at and feeling them.

Special support
Hold your own hand over the child's handprint. Whose hand is the biggest? Whose hand is the smallest?

Extension
Help the children to make greeting cards or collages with the sandy handprints. Alternatively, create a frieze of them all around a 'Welcome to nursery' sign.

LINKS WITH HOME
Use the hand-washing activity to introduce this new skill. Keep the parents or carers of the child that you are targeting in touch with progress so that they can encourage them to be more independent at home, too.

CREATIVE DEVELOPMENT • CREATIVE DEVELOPMENT

LEARNING OBJECTIVE FOR ALL THE CHILDREN
● to recognize and explore how sounds can be changed.

INDIVIDUAL LEARNING TARGET
● to discriminate and respond differently to 'high' and 'low' sounds.

Swanee whistles

Group size
Eight to ten children.

What you need
A swanee whistle that makes a sliding high-low note, or other instruments such as a glockenspiel, a keyboard, a mouth organ and so on; disinfectant wipes or facilities for washing blowing instruments.

What to do
Choose an instrument and invite the children to listen to the sound it makes as you play it. When it goes high, they should raise their hands up in the air. When it goes low, they should hold their hands down low. If the children find this concept difficult to grasp, demonstrate it to them first.

Start off slowly raising and lowering the note. When the children get more confident, catch them out by some quick changes.

Invite some of the less confident children to make the whistle sound for the rest of the group to respond to. Use a disinfectant wipe to keep mouthpieces clean and hygienic.

Special support
Ask an adult helper or another child to model and exaggerate the movements for the child that you are targeting to copy. Make sure that they have a turn to make the high and low sounds so that they can enjoy all the children taking their lead from them.

Extension
Invite the children to tell you if you are playing your tuned instrument high or low. Make high squeaky voices and low growly voices on the instrument and use these as effects at story time.

LINKS WITH HOME
Ask parents and carers to help their children find one thing that makes a high sound and one thing that makes a low sound at home. If they are suitable and small enough, ask them to bring them in to 'show and tell'.

Musical swaps

Group size
Eight to 20 children.

What you need
A selection of percussion instruments in a box, such as shakers, drums, triangles, clappers, claves, bells and so on; lively CD or tape; CD player or tape recorder.

What to do
Ask the children to sit on the floor in a circle. Pass around the box of instruments and invite each child to select one. Encourage older children to place it on the floor in front of the child and wait until all the children are ready before explaining what you are going to do.

Tell the children that when the music plays, they can play, too. When the music stops, they should stop, too. Ask them to pick up their instruments as you begin to play the music. After thirty seconds or so, stop the music. Praise the children for listening and stopping. Now call out the names of two children and ask them to swap their instruments. Continue with the music.

Repeat this several times, each time naming two children to swap over. If you have a very large group, name two pairs at a time to swap. In this way, everyone has a turn with at least two musical instruments.

Special support
If necessary, show and tell the child that you are targeting how to play their instrument. Provide them with hand-over-hand support to prompt them to begin if necessary.

Extension
Place the instruments in the centre of the circle. Each time the music stops, the children can exchange their instruments with one from the 'pool'. Use tuned instruments, for example, chime bars and xylophones, as well as percussion instruments.

LEARNING OBJECTIVES FOR ALL THE CHILDREN
- to explore how sounds can be changed
- to use their imagination in music.

INDIVIDUAL LEARNING TARGETS
- to beat a drum
- to shake a shaker
- to bang claves together.

LINKS WITH HOME
Encourage the parents or carers of the child that you are targeting to use simple shakers at home for their child to 'play along' with tunes on the radio or television.

**LEARNING
OBJECTIVE FOR ALL
THE CHILDREN**
● to explore colour,
texture, shape and
form in two
dimensions.

**INDIVIDUAL
LEARNING TARGET**
● to enjoy selecting
and applying paints.

Abstract art

Group size
All the children, one or two at a time.

What you need
Hard outside surface; large sheet of plastic; A1 sheets of good-quality paper; sticky tape; selection of paints; paint trays; paint pots; large paintbrushes; large paint rollers; wellington boots; aprons; bowls of warm soapy water; towels.

What to do
Carry out this activity on a sunny day. Before the children arrive, spread the large plastic sheet over a hard outside surface. Stick your sheets of A1 paper together by applying sticky tape to the side that you will not be painting. The final sheet should be as large as possible, but small enough for you to be able to display it on a wall indoors once it is finished. Make sure that the plastic floor covering is larger than the paper so that you need not worry about splashes and spills. Mix the paints into the pots and trays and place an assortment of paintbrushes and rollers on the plastic sheet. Ensure that the bowls of water and towels are nearby.

Help the children to put on the aprons. Invite them to experiment with a range of ways of applying the paint, for example, using different brushes, rollers, even wellington boots to print with. Encourage a wide use of colour and enjoy the abstract shapes and effects created. Ensure that every child contributes and that all the area of the paper is used. Talk to the children as they paint, sharing the colours and providing a commentary of their actions. Are they enjoying painting? Why?

LINKS WITH HOME
Suggest that parents and carers play a boot-printing game with their children at home, using a bowl of water, pairs of wellington boots and a paved area.

Special support
Encourage the children to use big movements with the paintbrushes and rollers in order to build up their confidence. Allow the child that you are targeting a free range of movements to express themselves as far as is possible.

Extension
Invite older and more able children to plan the colours and effects that they would like to express.

LEARNING OBJECTIVES FOR ALL THE CHILDREN
● to use their imagination in dance and movement
● to use their imagination in design.

INDIVIDUAL LEARNING TARGET
● to move feet to music.

Foot jive

Group size
Six to 16 children.

What you need
CD player or tape recorder; CD or tape of rock-and-roll music; glove puppets or sock puppets, for example, old adult socks decorated with button eyes and tufts of wool hair; adult helper to assist with the children's shoes and socks.

What to do
Encourage the children to sit down in a space and to remove their shoes and socks. Provide only as much help as is needed. Invite them to sit with their bare feet stretched out in front of them. Share the fun as you tell them that you are all going to teach your feet how to 'rock and roll'.

As you start the music, make your feet bob to the right and to the left, spring apart (ankles still together) and come back together again. Encourage the children to make up their own foot dance.

Now ask the children to put on their socks again, helping them if necessary. Invite each child to put a glove puppet or sock puppet onto their feet and encourage them to keep their ankles together as they make their puppet dance to the music. Stop and invite pairs of children to swap puppets. Have two or three turns of the 'foot puppet dance'.

Special support
Use this activity as a chance to teach independence. Have a 'backward chaining' approach to help the child that you are targeting to pull off their socks. First, pull the sock down to the toes and ask the child to pull the sock off. Then, in time, pull the sock down just to the ankle and ask the child to pull it off their foot. Gradually 'link the chains' backward until the child is performing the whole task.

Extension
Make simple sock puppets with the children to accompany this activity.

LINKS WITH HOME
Keep parents and carers informed of your activities so that they can practise the same dressing and undressing actions at home with their children.

Long boat

Group size
Six to 20 children.

What you need
An open floor space; adult helpers.

What to do
This is a 'long boat' version of the familiar rhyme 'Row, Row, Row Your Boat' (Traditional). You will find suggestions for the more familiar version in another book in this series, *Speech and Language Difficulties* in the activity 'Row the boat' on page 30.

Sit on the floor together in a long line. Encourage each child to sit with their legs apart, one each side of the child in front. If the line is long, have an extra helper at the front and one or two in the middle. Start by singing the traditional rhyme as you rock from side to side, steadying yourselves with a hand each side of you.

Row, row, row your boat,
Gently down the stream;
Merrily, merrily, merrily, merrily,
Life is but a dream.

Introduce new versions for the last two lines, then think of some more together. It does not matter if they do not rhyme or scan. Build them around the children's own ideas, for example, 'If you see a tall giraffe, don't forget to laugh' (everybody laugh); 'If you see a big baboon, don't forget to swoon' (everybody fall over to the 'oo' sound); 'If you see a prowling lion, don't forget to scream!' (everybody scream); 'If you see a hippopotamus, don't forget to make a lot of fuss!' (everybody cry). End with a final verse of the traditional rhyme. When the children's balance is steady enough, encourage them to move their arms in a rowing movement, first one arm, then the other, in synchrony.

Special support
Ask an adult to sit immediately behind the child that you are targeting to help their balance and to share the fun.

Extension
Encourage the children to help you make long boats with cardboard boxes and paddles. Climb into them and sing the rhyme as you 'row, row, row' together.

LEARNING OBJECTIVE FOR ALL THE CHILDREN
● to sing a simple song from memory and match movements to music.

INDIVIDUAL LEARNING TARGET
● to join in the repeated words of a familiar song.

LINKS WITH HOME
This is a good song to send home for the children to practise with their parents or carers. It can be used to distract the child that you are targeting at awkward times, for example, when getting dressed.

Sensational sculptures

Group size
Two or three children.

What you need
Open space; large cardboard boxes; empty packaging of many different shapes and sizes; glue; sheets of shiny coloured paper; scissors; large plastic sheet; photographs or postcards of large abstract sculptures; brightly coloured paints; paintbrushes; table.

What to do
Spread the large plastic sheet on the floor in the middle of an open space. Collect bits and pieces of packaging together and display them on the edge of the plastic sheeting. Place a table close by with shiny pieces of paper, scissors and glue. Add other large collage materials if you wish to.

Bring the children to your sculpture area and suggest that you make a giant floor sculpture together, using a range of shapes and materials. Show them the photographs or postcards so that they understand what a sculpture is and encourage them to talk about what they would like their sculpture to look like or contain. Look at the materials and select together the pieces to go at the bottom. Help the children to plan ahead, thinking of the kinds of shapes that they might need near the bottom and the details they would like to add near the top. Support the children as they cut, stick and shape their design. Invite them to paint the finished product in bright colours.

Special support
Help the child that you are targeting to plan ahead rather than add pieces randomly or by trial and error. Support their ideas by helping with the positioning and gluing.

Extension
Help the children to make more complex sculptures by covering folded chicken wire with papier mâché.

LEARNING OBJECTIVE FOR ALL THE CHILDREN
● to explore shape, form and space in three dimensions.

INDIVIDUAL LEARNING TARGET
● to plan what to do next.

LINKS WITH HOME
Transform your entrance lobby into a giant sculpture park and ask parents and carers to encourage their children to tell them about their sculptures.

LEARNING OBJECTIVE FOR ALL THE CHILDREN
● to recognize repeated sound patterns and match movements to music.

INDIVIDUAL LEARNING TARGET
● to start and stop playing to a visual signal.

Watch the conductor

Group size
All the children, with one adult to eight children.

What you need
A selection of percussion musical instruments; CD player or tape recorder; music CD or tape; adult helper.

What to do
Carry out this activity with those children who are familiar with the routines of a music session and used to both looking and listening. Choose the instruments that you would like the children to play. Give them out in sections so that all the children with shakers are next to one another, then the drums, then the jingle bells and so on.

Tell the children to watch very carefully because the conductor will show them when to start and when to stop playing their instruments. Introduce two hand signals – a downwards arm movement for 'start' and a policeman's halt signal for 'stop'. Practise starting and stopping to the conductor's signal.

Now explain to the children that the conductor will point to different groups of instruments and tell them when to start and stop. Ask the adult helper to start the tape or accompaniment and then signal to the drums, to the bells, to the shakers and so on when they are to join in and when they are to stop. Start by bringing the groups of instruments in gradually, have a central section with everyone taking part, then gradually fade the music as different sections drop out again. Praise the children for looking and listening.

Special support
Stay with the 'start' and 'stop' signals until the child that you are targeting is ready for more complex directions. Use a light touch to remind them to look, and praise all efforts.

LINKS WITH HOME
Encourage the parents or carers of the child that you are targeting to use a light touch and a name before giving their child simple instructions.

Extension
Copy the photocopiable sheet on page 95 onto a piece of card and cut it into four. Show the children the four symbols. Explain that conductors have their own special ways of telling musicians how to play. The large 'f' (for 'forte') means 'play loudly'. The small 'p' (for 'piano') means 'play softly'. The hairpin opening wider means 'play louder and louder', and the hairpin opening narrower means 'play softer and softer'. Use these symbols to conduct, adding your own gestures to remind the children what to do.

Individual education plan

Name:	Code of Practice Stage:

Nature of learning difficulty:

Action	Who will do what?
1. Seeking further information	
2. Seeking training or support	
3. Observations and assessments	
4. Encouraging learning and development	

What exactly are the new skills we wish to teach?

How will we teach them?

What opportunities will we make for helping the child to generalize and practise these skills throughout the session?

How will we make sure the child is fully included in the early years curriculum?

Help from parents or carers:

Targets for this term:

How will we measure whether we have achieved these?

Review meeting with parents or carers:

Who else to invite:

Half-termly play monitoring sheet

Name of child:	Date:

Play activity:

How does (s)he play with this activity at the moment?

What ways would we like to encourage him/her to play with this activity over the next few weeks?

How will we do this?

Review
How did it go?

Date:

SPECIAL NEEDS **in the early years:** Learning difficulties

Feeling Lotto

My needs

This is how I communicate

Name:	Date:

This is what I do when I need to attract a grown-up's attention
This is what I do when I need to draw your attention to another child or toys
This is how I ask for things
This is how I show that I am happy
This is how I show that I am unhappy or frightened
This is how I let you know that I've had enough of something
This is how I let you know when I need the toilet or need changing
This is what I do when I'm really interested in something
This is how I say 'goodbye'

SPECIAL NEEDS **in the early years:** Learning difficulties

Sticker snakes

Use coloured stickers or crayons to make the snakes look exactly the same.

Rice is nice

Time of day

Draw the hands on the clock-faces to show what a busy time you have had today.

This is the time when we arrive.

This is the time when we have our drinks.

This is the time when we play outside.

This is the time when we go home.

Wonderful windmills

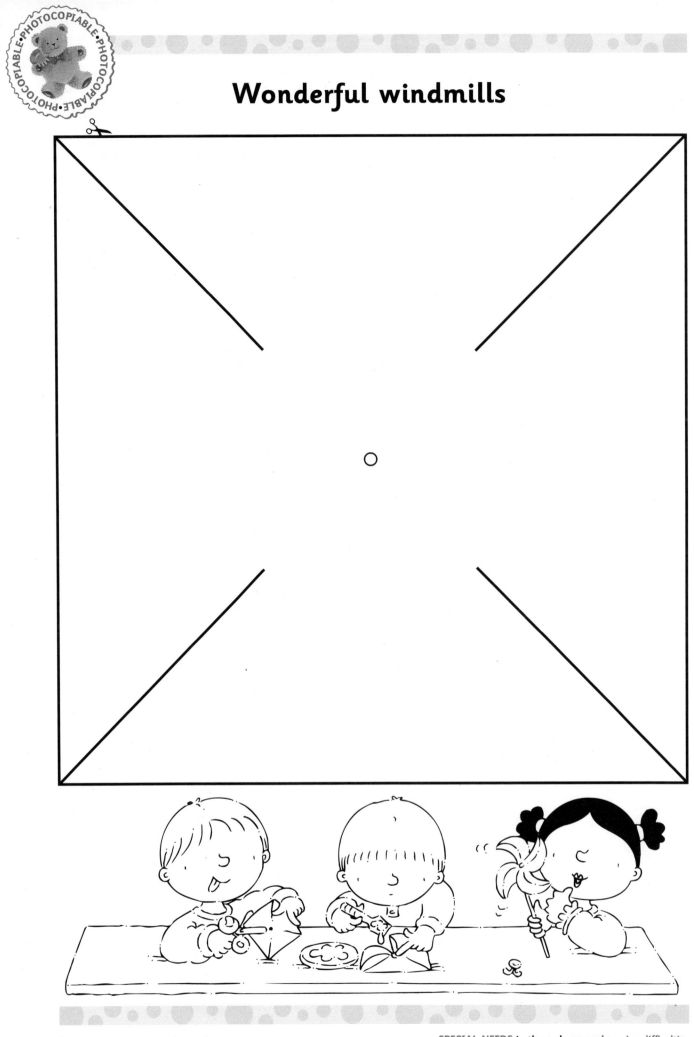

Harry Hedgehog

Out of my window

Out of my window
I can see
Cars and lorries
A tall green tree.

Out of my window
A red post van
A telephone box
And the ice-cream man.

Out of my window
Shops and flats
Traffic-lights
And a small black cat.

Brenda Williams

Watch the conductor

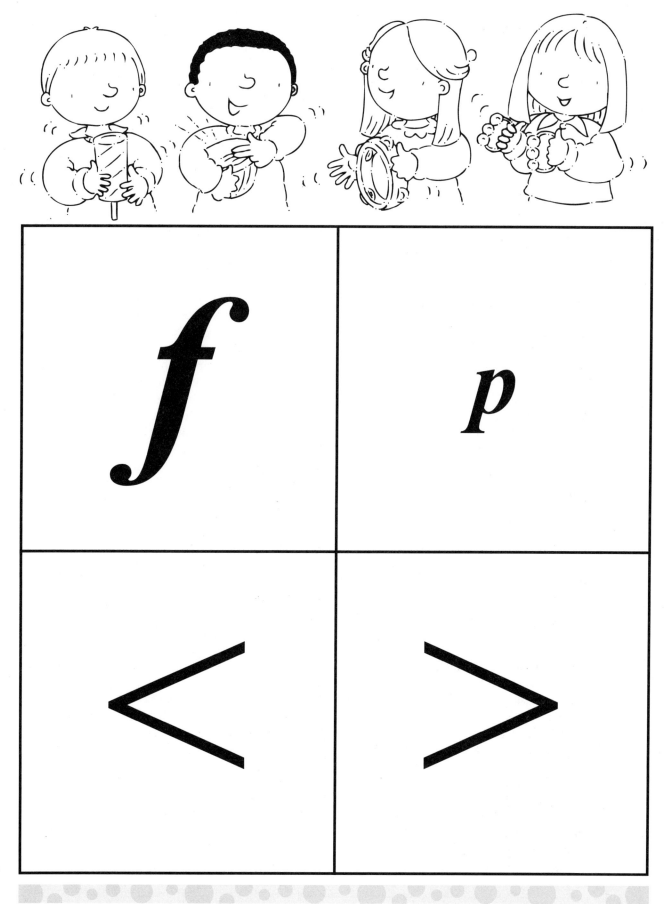

RECOMMENDED RESOURCES

ORGANIZATIONS AND SUPPORT GROUPS
● The *CaF Directory* of specific conditions and rare syndromes in children with their family support networks can be obtained on subscription from Contact a Family, 209-211 City Road, London, EC1V 1JN. Tel: 020-76088700.

BOOKS FOR ADULTS
● *Special Needs and Early Years Provision* by Hannah Mortimer (Continuum)
● *Learning in the Early Years* series of seven books, including *Ready for Inspection* by Pauline Kenyon (Scholastic)
● *What Works in Inclusive Education?* by Judy Sebba and Darshan Sachdev (Barnardo's)
● *All Together: How to Create Inclusive Services for Disabled Children and Their Families* by Mary Dickins (National Early Years Network)

WEBSITES
● The Department for Education and Employment (D*f*EE) (for parent information and for Government circulars and advice including the SEN *Code of Practice*): www.dfee.gov.uk
● The Down's Syndrome Association: www.dsa-uk.com
● MENCAP (support organization for children with severe learning difficulites and their families): www.mencap.org.uk
● The Writers' Press, USA, publish a number of books for young children about a range of SEN: www.writerspress.com

EQUIPMENT SUPPLIERS
● KCS, FREEPOST, Southampton SO17 1YA. Specialist tools for making computer equipment accessible to all children.
● National Association of Toy and Leisure Libraries, 68 Churchway, London NW1 1LT. Tel: 020-73879592. Publish the *Playsense* pack.
● Step by Step, Lee Fold, Hyde, Cheshire SK14 4LL. Tel: 0845-3001089. Supply toys for all special needs.
● Acorn Educational Ltd, 32 Queen Eleanor Road, Geddington, Kettering, Northants. NN14 1AY. Tel: 01536-400212. Supply equipment and resources for pre-school early years and special needs.
● LDA Primary and Special Needs, Duke Street, Wisbech, Cambridgeshire PE13 2AE. Tel: 01945-463441.
● *Playladders* checklist by Hannah Mortimer (Quality for Effective Development). Available from QEd, The Rom Building, Eastern Avenue, Lichfield WS13 6RN. Tel: 01543-416353.

ORGANIZATIONS THAT PROVIDE TRAINING COURSES
● Makaton Vocabulary Development Project, 31 Firwood Drive, Camberley, Surrey GU15 3QD. Tel: 01276-671368. Information about Makaton sign vocabulary and training.
● National Portage Association, PO Box 3075, Yeovil, Somerset BA21 3FB. Tel: 01935-471641. For Portage carers and workers, for training in Portage and for information on the 'Quality Play' training.
● National Children's Bureau, 8 Wakley Street, London EC1V 7QE. Tel: 020-7843 6000. Many seminars and workshops on children and SEN.
● Pre-school Learning Alliance National Centre, 69 Kings Cross Road, London WC1X 9LL. Tel: 020-78330991. Information on DPP courses and their special needs certificate. Free catalogue, order form and price list of publications available.
● National Early Years Network, 77 Holloway Road, London N7 8JZ. Tel: 020-76079573. For customized in-house training.
● National Association for Special Educational Needs (NASEN), 4–5 Amber Business Village, Amber Close, Amington, Tamworth, Staffordshire B77 4RP. Tel: 01827-311500. For publications and workshops on all aspects of SEN.
● Children in Scotland, Princes House, 5 Shandwick Place, Edinburgh EH2 4RG. Tel: 0131-2288484. Courses in early years including SEN.
● The Sarah Duffen Centre, Belmont Street, Southsea, Hampshire PO5 1NA. Tel: 023-92824261. Workshops and courses on young children with Down's syndrome.